DANGEROUS AFFIRMATIONS

Dangerous Affirmations: My Transgender Experience

Copyright © 2021 Help 4 Families

Published in the United States of America.

ISBN: 978-1-7365951-2-1 (paperback)

DANGEROUS AFFIRMATIONS

MY

TRANSGENDER

EXPERIENCE

JERRY LAKE

with Denise Shick

A Special Thanks

You who had offered yourself and your pain in order to help others
we thank you. We wish to extend to each of you our gratitude. May
the Lord bless your lives beyond what you could ever imagine.

Contents

Foreword

Jerry Lake demonstrates great courage choosing to share and speak of his personal experience of believing he should have been female. He is not alone in having these feelings. They are rooted in the desire to fix his deep emotional wounds. Sadly, many are lost in their true identity and attempt to escape reality.

Throughout Jerry's story, you will read from his personal diary entries and understand firsthand how he and others decided that being someone else was so appealing to them. You will read through each one's experiences that give reasons for their desire to be some-one else.

It may be further helpful to clarify some terminology used in Jerry's personal story. Though the limit of definition is applied primarily to the male, the female can readily make direct comparison.

Language and definitions have changed much throughout the last ten years through activists and people's desire to be labeled. It will be helpful to know the history of terms used within *Dangerous Affirmations*.

Transvestite was previously used to describe a man who was content to episodically cross-dress, primarily for the sexual excitement and momentary emotional relief it brought through masturbation, through visual stimulations, and through peaked excitement, with its resultant sense of feeling peaceful and calm.

Cross-dressing and **tranvestism** were essentially the same: Cross-dressing and transvestism were simply two titles ascribed to one behavior. The terms could be defined as an attraction to wear the clothing of the opposite sex in order to achieve sexual stimulation, arousal, and emotional/sexual pleasure—in order to escape one's own self-despised identity, stress, and daily reality, if but for a few minutes of duration.

Transvestism was the first of many steps toward what typically became a regularly practiced, increasingly addictive, and compulsive means to momentarily medicate one's inner emotional pain. In effect, the man momentarily took upon himself the outward inner-emotional healing, and sexual relief became a habitual form of sexually addictive behaviors, wherein the man was temporarily able to become both the male and the female, bypassing any need to become intimately associated with a real woman.

In 2021, **transgender** or **trans-gender** is the term used to define the individual who feels steadily more incongruent in his or her God-given gender role (and sexual identity), feeling it is increasingly imperative to be dressed-up because of the immediate emotional and sexual relief doing so brings. There is often a "psychotic-break" with one's real, birth-given identity, resulting in eventual attempts to rectify the distorted self-view through irreversible, surgical amputation of an otherwise healthy, viable human appendage. This is called **Sex-Reassignment Surgery (SRS)**. The battle-fatigued soldiers who have been blown apart by the cluster bomb called transgender are those who feel totally out of place living within their God-given gender role. There is a growing disconnect with being forced to live as a member of their God-given gender and it may be abandoned altogether. Identifying as transgender is usually something that progresses in its development.

I pray *Dangerous Affirmations* is helpful and brings a better under-standing of the real struggle behind the scenes of the hurting.

—**DENISE SHICK**, author and founder of Help 4 Families

Introduction

There are abundant materials available that support transgender dysphoria (confusion), usually called transgender. This resource is meant to be a basic primer on beginning to understand what actually causes such problems. It is not a scholastic, clinical research project. There is little on the secular or Christian market that offers a hopeful resolution to the otherwise lifelong and crippling effects of these forms of human brokenness. The pendulum too often swings to either extreme: legalistic intolerance or the equally intolerant message of the pro-transgender activities.

I call your attention to the intolerance in both camps. It is easy to throw hand grenades or lob demeaning slogans at each other, but not so easy to bring resolution to the reasons for the conflict. Too much politicizing only prolongs the war.

One very important matter is overlooked when so actively involved in heated political debate over the "rightness" or "wrongness" of gender-identity matters: the person. Political agendas do not rescue the wounded and dying. I'm deeply concerned about the volatile relational missiles that produce such visceral wounds in one's basic sexual/gender identity. The core of this book addresses the psychological, spiritual, and social questions surrounding these issues, while keeping the wounded and dying in central focus.

I understand and appreciate the fact that I've already taken the risk of alienating some readers by suggesting that any of the conditions I've identified are considered to be a form of deviant behavior. Our society has strayed so far from the norm that we have little comprehension of how very abnormal many of us are in today's world.

Then, to make matters worse, I dare to suggest the possibility that all of this can have a redemptive fix. "How naïve!" say the scoffers.

Then there are those readers who cannot comprehend how a Christian (in my case) would ever wrestle with such desires to begin with. These folks would seriously question the authenticity of my salvation experience, while it's really a reflection of my refusal to become sanctified and cleansed from the iniquity-drive within my soul.

As one evangelist put it:

> "It's not that you are broken and need something
> fixed as much as it is that you have been fixed and
> were not broken."

—*Jerry Lake*

Chapter 1

How Did I Get Here?

How can I ever do without my daily routine of cross-dressing? It's entirely too painful to think of the horror of quitting. I cannot possibly survive without this, my source of life, purpose, satisfaction and sense of well-being! Don't even suggest that I cut this out of my daily diet, you well-meaning religionists or ignorant therapist. No way! I'll die without it! I've got to live . . . and the only way I can survive is as the woman I should have been.

—Carol Ann

Changing Seasons

I could see my reflection in the windowpane of the doctor's office. I had wanted to see this psychiatrist for a long time. I loathed going to a male shrink and had conducted an exhaustive search, which finally led me to Dr. Nancy. I saw her as an answer to my lifelong prayer, for she was my first step toward achieving sex-reassignment surgery. Dr. Nancy had made a special request on the phone that I come to her office dressed as the woman I wanted to be. My excitement skyrocketed as I prepared myself for the appointment. I was out to win an Oscar in this performance!

But now, as I waited to see her, I felt growing apprehension. What if she was not sufficiently impressed to cooperate with my plan? In my nervousness, I managed to bite off my lipstick. A moment later, with a fresh application of Avon's best and an added touch of Timeless perfume, I was ready for my appointment.

The receptionist interrupted my thoughts. "Carol, the doctor is ready to see you now."

I glanced out of the window and saw the trees turning from green to shades of flaming red. This was my change of season. I told myself, *At last!* The receptionist led me down the hall to an office with a distinctively feminine décor. In the far corner was a wicker chair with a striking floral design. I positioned myself in it as gracefully as possible, making certain my legs were crossed at just the right angle. Sheila came in and greeted me warmly, using my female name as though it was absolutely normal. I found this to be very gratifying! Minutes later, in my best, practiced falsetto, I began recounting my story to this empathetic, attentive woman.

She sat on the edge an adjacent couch and leaned forward within a few inches of me, conversing, *woman to woman,* occasionally placing a comforting hand on my mine. She listened, probed, questioned. Helping herself to another cup of coffee, she remarked, "I love your dress," and then began to tell me that I made a very attractive woman. (*Glory!*) "I wish I could look half as nice," she sighed, and then she paused and asked, "Carol, when did you first begin to cross-dress?"

I Was Only Four . . .

I thought back to the age of four, when I contracted polio. Cross-dressing was already a big part of my life by then. My sexual assignment must have been messed up in the womb—at least that was how I reasoned. She agreed.

As we talked about my lifetime of pain, I reached into my purse for more tissue. I hadn't planned to cry so much, and I didn't want to my mascara to run. "I'm making a fool of myself, aren't I?" I asked.

"Not at all," she assured me. Then Dr. Nancy read aloud the journal entry I'd sent her a few days before:

> "I feel so stupid—and inadequate to fulfill the role
> of a male. I feel that I am out of place in this body,
> this time in history, this sexual identity. I cannot feel
> differently about myself. I am predominantly female in
> my innermost thoughts and feelings. I have come to feel
> nothing but intense hatred for manhood! Sometimes
> (like today) I nearly go crazy thinking about once
> again being dressed in women's clothing and living as
> Carol Anne.
>
> "I can't wait to once again see her (Carol's) reflection in
> the mirror. I have lived too long in this daily torment
> of being a woman and having to function as a man.
> I have tried to put an end to my feelings, but I cannot.
> I simply want to be honest about how I feel. I want
> so much to be at peace with who I feel myself to be:

WOMAN! I hate manhood! I cannot tolerate having male sex organs or the feelings that are associated with having them. The incessant drive to obtain orgasm is repulsive to me. I renounce masculinity, removing everything in my world that has anything to do with being a male. I hate men and even more, I hate being numbered among them. Deplorable!

"I will as Carol, think, feel, behave—to be her in every conceivable way! I hate, detest, loathe, disdain, despise, reject, abhor, denounce, turn away from completely, and once and for all remove from my mind the entrapments of manhood. Manhood is not for me! There is nothing short of suicide that will deter me from this lifelong goal. I will be Carol, even if it kills me. I can no longer concern myself about how others feel. I must be the woman I am supposed to be. The ache I have inside of never being able to express who I really am is almost more than my mind can any longer endure. It is too painfully unjust. I did not ask for this! I have tried, but have discovered that life is not worth living as a man. Manhood just does not fit me!"

As I had hoped, Dr. Nancy's maternal instincts surfaced as she cupped my hands into hers. "You poor dear; I don't understand why you've gone through all of this torment, but soon you will be feeling much better." Then she began writing a prescription. My heart leaped! "This medication must be taken just as directed," she said firmly. "You will begin to notice some physical changes in a few months. Be patient."

Later, when the pharmacist handed me the bag containing my dream-come-true drugs, my hands shook almost uncontrollably with excitement. It would just be a matter of time before my body would begin its metamorphosis.

Consulting with a sex-change therapist and beginning to take female hormones—all of it seemed so right. There was just one problem. I was a married man, a father, and a Christian leader.

My Closest Friends

Since my earliest memories, my closest friends had been females who had accepted me as one of their own. This was coupled with the disturbing realization that having a son had not been my parents' first choice.

"I wish you would have been a girl so that you could one day take over my beauty shop," my mother often mused.

When, as a six-year-old, I played dress up with the little girls in the neighborhood, my father would say, teasingly, "Hey, Jerry, you're a lot better looking as a girl."

Unintentionally, my parents' remarks left a deep impression, and wounds of rejection took deep roots in my soul. It was not that they didn't love me—they did. They were just ignorant of the impact of their words on their young son.

Clay McLean explained in his lecture on Gender Identity Development:

> "Both men and women's gender identity come from our prelateship with our earthly father. It is our father who tells us that we are women or men. It is the father who is to come and stand between our mother and us. We don't know that we are to be separated from mothers; we are born of her and do not know that we are to be someone separate from her unless someone tells us. And it's not the mother who can really or effectively tell us that. It has to be that "other voice," other than the feminine voice, to speak to that little boy or girl and come between the mother and the child and help them discover themselves outside of their relationship with their mother.

> "A girl child is a potential woman, but she needs to learn about her own unique identity, separate from her mother, though she does not have to be separate from her, for she is a woman. The boy child has to learn that he totally separate from his mother. So, without his father's loving voice to come in and separate him from his mother, he remains connected to her. It's not that the father says, 'Come here right now' or 'come here, boy, because I am going to make a man out of you.' No, this is not how it happens. In fact, that actually keeps it from happening. It happens by loving him away from his mother into his world, thereby imparting to

him his own masculine identity. When the boy has not had that happen, he spends the rest of his life trying to find a man that will do that. That is not just true of the homosexuals. You can spend your entire life looking for the boss who will treat you like a son or the older man or the minister who will treat you like your daddy."[1]

Teenage Animosity Toward Father

By the time I was a teenager, the bond between Dad and me was nonexistent. And then one night any remaining fragile connection was finally completely severed. I'd been sick with the flu and had gone to bed early. Later that evening Dad unexpectedly came into my bedroom to check on me. I say unexpectedly because it was something that he'd never done as far as I can recollect. I remember hearing the sound of his footsteps coming down the hallway and then stopping outside my door.

No, it couldn't be! As I heard the turn of the doorknob, I quickly closed my eyes and began breathing deeply. As Dad leaned over my bed, the light from the hallway fell across my face, revealing my well-kept secret: the red lips, the eyelashes thick with mascara, the lace at my neckline. I heard him suck in his breath and then let out a moan. I felt his heavy frame slump down at the foot of my bed. I lay there motionless, listening to his muffled sobs.

Then, as abruptly as it had begun, the sobbing stopped. The next thing I knew I was being yanked out of bed as Dad unleashed his

---

1 Clay Mclean Lecture on "Gender Identity Disorder": 1989.

pain in blow after blow to my chest, my groin, and my face. "You're a damned homosexual!" he yelled over and over.

Mom came running into the room, sobbing and screaming for Dad to stop. That was all it took. Dad couldn't bear the sight of the love of his life crying. She led him out of the room and the door clicked behind them. Then another door clicked shut—the door to my heart. Never again would Dad have access to it; the risk was too great. From that point on, I did everything I could to distance myself from him and suppress the part of me that still desperately longed for his love and affirmation.

Survival was the all-consuming thing. Being around Dad threatened my very sense of being. Something had happened! The damage was permanent and severe. Contrary to what my father assumed, at that time I was not sexually attracted to men. In fact, I came to harbor an intense dislike, if not a hatred, for men and anything to do with being one of them. In contrast, I loved being in the company of females. You could say that the homosexual constantly is engaged in his *fight from women*, while the transgender is consumed in his *flight toward women*.

However, following Dad's angry outburst, I began to question if perhaps I really was a homosexual. (Oh, the incredible power of the spoken word.) I tried to fantasize what it would be like to be in relationship with a man, finally concluding that such a possibility would take form only if I were a woman.

Charles Williams' *Descent into Hell* reveals the effects of a man's choices to fabricate a woman to love. This imaginary woman eventually consumes every thought, the illusion becoming progressively more captivating and the descent into hell all the more a reality:

"a form of a shape went out and he was drawn, steadingly inward and down through the bottomless circles of the void."[2]

Internal conflict about my sexual/gender identity continued throughout my high school years. I dated several girls only to discover that doing so stirred more envy within me; I longed to be like them. My desire to spend more time in the presence of females escalated. I enjoyed being among the girls.

Eventually I found one girl who let me cross-dress in her presence. That was thrilling. Cross-dressing became a daily preoccupation—an obsession. I always felt like such a weirdo! Unending fantasies filled the galleries of my imagination. Life as a male became increasingly intolerable, but I managed to keep my secret. Only the girls who were close to me knew it was a deep desire. I'm sure my mother was in great turmoil, not knowing what to do with her wayward, sullen son, probably feeling that she was responsible for my condition.

Soldier Up!

Upon graduation from high school, I enlisted in the military in the vain hope that perhaps that experience would usher me into real manhood. It did not.

After completing fourteen months of service as a hospital corpsman, I nervously made an appointment with the base psychiatrist in order to see what could be done about my inner turmoil. Two weeks later I was honorably discharged. The psychiatrist explained it this way: "We simply don't know what to do with people like you. Obviously, we cannot give you the help you require. We are giving

---

2 Charles Williams, *Descent into Hell*, p.192.

you a discharge so you can return home to get the professional help you need."

Although my parents were made fully aware of the nature of my problem and the reasons for my discharge, they never once discussed the subject with me. I suppose they just hoped for the best. They bore their pain privately—as did I. This "family secret" stayed within the family.

In another attempt to find meaning, I enrolled in a nearby Christian college, upon the recommendation of our pastor. It was there that I met a vibrantly alive young Christian woman who would later walk down the isle with me. Prior to our engagement I mentioned my struggles to her, using terminology that I know was terribly inaccurate, labeling myself a transgender. Elizabeth did not even know what the word meant. Understandably, she did not realize the depth of my problem; we were naïve and thought marriage would be the ultimate remedy. We didn't understand that it was not a sexual problem but rather a festering core-identity issue. Little did we realize the severity of the wounding or the deep pool of pain hidden within my heart.

Marriage: The Cure?

To our mutual disappointment, even after marriage and a normal sexual relationship, my secret obsession continued to harass me, and, in turn, my wife. I would secretly dress up when she was gone from home. Often I would feign sickness so that I could be home all day to once again invite into our bedroom my "other love": Carol Ann.

As my passion to be recognized as a woman intensified, I would chronically act out my hidden desires, often taking unbelievable risks by exposing myself as Carol in public places. I frequented dangerous areas late at night. It's a miracle of God's protective care that I was not arrested or picked up by some sex-craved man and discarded as a piece of worthless refuse in some ditch.

One day during our first year of marriage I let Elizabeth walk in on me at home when I was cross-dressed. I had concocted the whole discovery, planning on convincing her to agree with me to engage in that behavior, just as long as it remained between us and in the privacy of our home. *After all, it's not hurting anyone, and it's a necessary emotional outlet. It would be our secret,* I reasoned.

Needless to say, the idea did not fly! But I did—out the door and into the car until I could come back home looking like the man she had married. I promised her that I would abstain if it upset her so much. I vowed I'd never do it again. Thus began the routine cycle of promises and assurances that would ultimately be broken over and over for the next twenty years of living a double life. I often felt like an espionage agent hiding my second life, always strategizing, concealing private stashes of clothing—always covering my tracks.

I expended a lot of emotional and physical energy and caused great torment for both of us. Of course, I eventually began to seriously consider the possibility of sex-reassignment surgery (SRS). Like any form of lust, the deceptions became more complex and involved, leading me down a path of self-destruction I never thought possible. I was missing one vital piece of wisdom, which we transgenders usually ignore:

> "Secret, repetitive sin becomes a taskmaster rather
> than a pleasure. You may have comforted yourself
> so far with the notion that you are getting away

with it . . . but count on it—as long as anything in your life continues to be uncontrollable, you are in bondage to it. For now, the bondage itself is its own consequence."[3]

All the while I reasoned that God fully understood and accepted my plight and perhaps, out of His compassionate love, even condoned my behavior and the decisions I was making. After all, it was His "oversight" that brought on the whole condition in the first place, right?

Looking at my reflection in the expanse of glass before me, I thought I looked very pretty. I am standing here, not in the self-conscious way of a man encircled by women, but as one miraculously transformed to be accepted as another woman among them, not as a male intrusion. A mixture of feelings quickly ceased as I saw the façade and caught a glimpse of my inner man beneath the carefully constructed exterior, muttering in contempt, "It is true, neither sex is mine. I belong to a third sex, one that has not yet been named."

Cross-Dressing and Addictive Cycles

Cross-dressing is a powerfully addictive means of coping with unresolved, internal pain. It became my daily escape from an intense self-hatred and the stress of being forced into carrying out what had become to me the worst role ever—that of a man. The popular

---

3 Joe Dallas, *Desires in Conflict*, (Harvest House, 1991), 27.

saying "Love the sinner; hate the sin," became for me, "Love the sin; hate the sinner." Self-contempt had rooted itself within me.

I recently spoke with a man whose present situation is like an echo from my past. He described it this way:

> "I feel like I'm strapped to the front end of
> runaway locomotive, incapable of doing
> anything to change the course that is leading
> to certain disaster, I realize that I'm totally
> selfish in cross-dressing and contemplating sex
> reassignment, but the compulsion is entirely
> too strong for me to resist. I don't know how to
> get the train off of this awful track."

I believe the crux of the issue is becoming self-absorbed rather than allowing God to have His rightful place of loving authority in our lives. We enter into a revelation of sorts, demanding that God alter His plan and give us permission to proceed in mediating our pain according to our plan.

Harry Schaumburg elucidates:

> "As addicts seek to create their own meaning in life,
> to produce a sensation of potency, and actively
> to challenge a hostile environment that brings
> overwhelming feelings of and helplessness, they
> become self-reliant. They depend on what they can
> do for themselves rather than on what God can
> do for and through them. They create patterns of
> behavior that allow them to maintain pleasurable
> state of being rather than admitting that they can't
> cope with their problems and turning to God and

others for help. In short, they arrogantly believe they can solve their problems on their own . . . that fulfillment life can be self-created. Unfortunately, when people seek a 'taste of heaven' by their own means they create a living hell of uncontrolled desires. A hell of unremitting anguish that demands moments of illusory relief through more sexual behavior and the fantasy."[4]

Perhaps a conflict would arise at work, and I'd feel that I'd failed again. *You're stupid*, I would think. *You will never amount to anything; you would have gotten that promotion if you were a woman.*

Driving home in downtown traffic, I would notice a woman crossing the street. The swing of her hips and the swish of her dress was all it would take to tantalize me with thoughts of how her attire would look and feel on me. Soon I would be heading for a nearby mall to purchase some women's clothing and a stylish wig, along with the necessary cosmetics to complete the transformation. Within the privacy of a motel room, I'd go through the process of once more becoming the self I loved. It always felt as if I'd finally come home. I would once again breathe a deep sigh of relief.

Many times I went out for a long walk or drive, perhaps even to a mall to do some shopping as Carol Ann. I'd spent a lifetime practicing the finer art of walking with feminine flair and carrying myself like the women I had so admired (idolized?), especially my mother. I felt a rush of excitement when clerks called me "ma'am," or other female customers accepted me as just another woman like themselves. Once back in the motel, my fantasies would peak as

---

4 Harry Schaumburg, *False Intimacy*, (Navpress, 1997), 66.

I finally stimulated myself to a sexual orgasm. Eventually the whole experience would have to end, and I would once again be forced to resume my hated existence as a man. Typically, I'd then discard the new clothes in a Salvation Army deposit box on my dreaded trip back home. Feelings of shame, guilt, frustration, and anger would overwhelm me—and I'd promise myself that I'd never cross-dress again. But a few days, weeks, or months later the cycle would be repeated.

Dr. Nancy

Finally, in an attempt to resolve my inner turmoil, I made the appointment with Dr. Nancy in order to obtain female hormones. I dreamed of having transgender "corrective" surgery and becoming a woman—full time! I even forged a phony divorce certificate to hide the fact that I was still married. But, during a much later session, I tearfully told the doctor how apprehensive I was about actually going through the sex reassignment. It had nothing to do with the pain of surgery. The anguish that gripped my heart came as a result of having had honest dialogue with many postoperative transgenders about their "new life." Remarkably, they were still wrestling with unresolved emotional conflicts and psychological problems. They were still in therapy and still very angry or disappointed with God—and life. Most troublesome of all, they were involved in homosexual or bisexual relationships, prostitution, or sadomasochism. Their social circle was very narrow. They had not gone on with life. How could that be?

Creating an Illusion

How well I remember my first encounter with a postoperative transgender. I sat in absolute shock, listening to the woman who confessed her regrets in choosing to live as a man. She had the appearance of a young, rather effeminate but athletic male. She showed me pictures of what she had looked like before her new "reality." The photographs revealed what would have been my idyllic dream. She'd once been attractive and feminine, with long brunette hair.

She told me about her overall dissatisfaction—especially since becoming a Christian—in her altered body.

> "My Lord has told me that what I've done is not really the answer. I believe it's against God's design for my life."

She admitted she'd been foolish; she referred to herself as a freak because of her own arrogant rebellion. She was suffering additional emotional wounds due to her grievously poor choices. Through the window of her eyes, I saw the deep anguish within.

Another meeting was equally disconcerting. The man wanted me to call him by his adopted female name, Andrea. It seemed appropriate since he had lived in that role for many years. He pulled off the illusion quite well, though his makeup was a bit too lavish and his mannerisms overplayed. Nevertheless, the person standing there typified the woman I had covetously desired to be for as long as I could remember.

His statement shook me mightily. Through a well-practiced falsetto, he confessed:

> "I didn't realize I'd be so torn inside, still having
> to listen to the inner cries of boyhood. I thought
> the surgery would take care of all that, but I still
> have to cope with my wounded masculine stuff,
> the same anger and rejection I faced as a boy.
> I still see life from a guy's point of view. I cannot
> escape myself, my real self. What do I do now?"

He summarized his plight in one word: foolishness! What I had envisioned as the epitome of personal fulfillment was nothing more to him than an illusion, a terrible unending cosmic joke of some sort and an attempt to play God by creating an alternate gender identity.

Nothing's Changed

A very good friend of mine shared some of his journey.

> "Nothing's really changed. I'm still dealing with
> the pain of not being loved, and now my family
> is rejecting me. My dad has now totally rejected
> me. That's what hurts the most, because
> I always thought he'd love me if I were a female."

Tim shared:

> "The dressing up seems to tickle my needs, but
> it never truly satisfies them. I have so enjoyed
> passing as a woman and having the total free-

dom to now live as one, but I'm finding that the enjoyment is beginning to wear off. With all my dreams now fulfilled, I'm wondering what I've really missed in reaching my potential as a man. I know it's crazy to wonder about that now, but it's what now consumes my thoughts. I'm now increasingly aware of the Holy Spirit convicting me of my wrongdoing in using dressing as a woman as a counterfeit means of satisfying that place that only He should fill. Now that I've given my whole heart to Jesus Christ, He has given me a new desire to quit being deceptive and rebellious against God. He has asked me to make Him the center of my life. I have decided to go back to living as a man again!"

I had to ask myself, *Could it be true that putting on a dress every day will eventually become as humdrum as putting on trousers and sports shirt? Is it possible that the real issues I try so desperately to escape will be lurking around the same corners even if people call me a woman?*

But I would not allow myself to listen to such a possibility. I consistently ignored the legitimate question, which begged an honest reply. As Proverbs 6:27 asks, "Can a man scoop fire into his lap and not burn his clothes?" But I allowed the incessant demands of my own desires to drown out common-sense answers and sound biblical instructions. In the courtroom of my mind, the merciless interrogator of my soul rebuffed any biblical arguments or sound rationale.

Posed behind her microphone, this wizened prosecutor proudly presented her closing argument. She would snarl, "Yes, yes, we hear the supposed truth of Scripture and all its ancient demands, but what about the fact that the gender switch remains so delectable, so inviting and tantalizing? Come on! To thyself be true! Is it not true that you would rather be a woman? Evidence to the contrary be damned!"

My confused mind swirled. I wanted to defend the personal experiences of those who had discovered that sex-reassignment surgery was not the answer. I wanted to defend myself in order to emphatically deny the erroneous charge that I would choose to play the role of a fool.

I would blurt out my sudden admission of guilt, "Yes, yes, yes! You are right. I think it would be better if I were a woman."

The prosecutor smugly sat down with a condescending glance in my direction. This seasoned trial lawyer had once again won her case by backing the guilty defendant into the corner of his own desires. "Guilty as charged!"

Shame

Brian, a former transgender, said,

> "One word keeps catching my attention: *shame*.
> Cross-dressing appeals to me, and its shameful-
> ness has been stuck in my mind."

Patrick Carnes says in his book *Don't Call It Love* that I'm ashamed of the things I do and I do the things I do to relieve the pain of the shame. I'm trapped in a non-ending cycle of shame. He lists occasions when I'm likely to feel shame, and some of them are true, such as when I sense being judged by others, or when past actions haunt me, or when I feel unlovable.

I need to be aware of situations in which these feelings arise and realize that the addict within is trying to draw me back into compulsive behaviors. Then, especially, I need to draw close to God and to my wife and others who know me and will stand with me. My goals are to do without any more forms of cross-dressing, masturbation, and sexual relations with anyone other than my wife—and to quit wearing any women's clothing or makeup, or of walking and or talking like a woman.

To help accomplish these goals, Carnes suggests listing boundaries I can set in place to avoid these destructive behaviors. For me, these boundaries must be:

- No visiting transgender or pornographic Internet sites

- No watching TV shows or movies with women wearing revealing clothing

- Turning away from magazine, TV, and newspaper ads for women's underwear, lingerie, and dresses

- No fantasizing about being a woman and wearing provocative clothing

- No flirtation with women other than my wife

- No staring at myself in the full-length mirror while I'm nude

- No sizing up women, or fantasizing what their experiences would be like in me

Two Minds

At this time, however cross-dressing had become my means of survival. To be immersed in womanhood had become my passion. I no longer wanted to live as a humdrum male. In order to escape that horrible fate, I wanted to move aside anything that might stand in my way and totally yielded to my fantasy, imagining what it would be like to be a woman. I desired to be transported into that more appealing realm where fantasies serve as "magic carpets to deliver my soul from boredom, anxiety, anger, loneliness, and rage to a 'better' work that offers momentary relief and satisfaction."[5]

Although I knew giving in was undoubtedly not going to be a panacea, lust propelled me.

> "The effort to possess another in order to steal enough passion to be lifted out of our current struggles into a world that feels (for an instant) like the Garden of Eden."[6]

But the same God who pursed Adam and Eve as they hid in their darkness would not leave me alone in mine. After some months on the hormones, I nervously informed my psychiatrist that I'd noticed few physical changes, and I told her of my fear of facing rejection. Then I added that the stories I'd heard from those who regretted their sex-reassignment surgery had caused me some real concern.

Dr. Nancy stood up and crossed the room, pointing her finger in my direction. "Carol, I cannot supply anymore hormones if you have no intention of following through with the procedure." She was further disheartened as she then read aloud my journal entry:

---

5 Dan Allender, *Bold Love*, (NavPress, 1992), 73.
6 Ibid, 103.

I am a Christian and married. I am a heterosexual.
I cannot pick up and go to Trinidad for sex reassignment. I know instinctively that surgical intervention
will not really eradicate the deeper issue in my soul. Of
course I have a skilled surgeon who assures me that he
can change my outward physical appearance, but what
about the manhood, my gender? Who can change that?
I find manhood unbearable. I want so much to be female.
I want to be forever done with the male sex drive.
Today I cross-dressed on four different occasions
in order to get the relief I required. It was good to
see myself once again draped in feminine softness. As
I write this, I am wearing a slip and pantyhose beneath
my sweat suit. My body is completely shaved, and my
elation is at its peak, even partially dressed as a female.
It goes entirely too deep. Why was I born this way, with
these male sex organs? This is indescribable anguish. I am
a woman! I want to be who I am! This double life is not
worth living. But how do I fulfill my demands and not
lose every human relationship I love so much? There lies
an insurmountable obstacle. I cannot be male, but I don't
know how to really be a female. In fact, I can't really
be a woman. I can only pretend. Is that good enough?
I don't think so.

My empathetic psychiatrist was losing patience with me. Nor was
she willing to continue seeing me until I resolved the matter. She
was not willing to stand with me on the shifting sands of my indeci-

sion. She said I was making her nervous. "Carol, you must make up your mind. Otherwise you'll make a fool out of both of us."

The drive home was a nightmare. Angry and terrified, I cursed my very existence. I tore at my dress, agonizing over my fate. For the rest of my life I would be forced to go through the motions of being a man, always fantasizing about what it would have been like . . . *if only.*

Back home I stepped into the shower, weeping and crying out to God for some relief. I had been a professing Christian for many years. My secret life was painful, not only to me and my beloved wife but also to my Savior. But as I stood there, letting the water wash away my tears, I also knew I was not ready to let it go. With or without hormones, Carol Anne was still alive, and I was not about to sign off on her divorce papers.

Fully dressed and enjoying the sight of my feminine persona now reflected in the mirror, I once again turned my back on my Creator's patient prompting. From my perspective, I had a clear rationale for what I was doing. I was Carol. As I viewed myself from all angles, I repeated over and over, "I'm a woman! I'm a woman!"

I wrote in my journal:

> I cannot conceive of ever doing without my cross-dressing. The very thought of ending it is too painful. How can I ever survive without this source of life, purpose, satisfaction and sense of well-being? Many times when I came home from an exhausting day and cross dressed, I consumed the excitement like food for my soul.

Immediate gratification had become my God, and I knew it. That was the snag in the whole deal. I knew too much about the true God. I knew I was out of His will while making fleshly bargains with the devil.

> *People will be lovers of themselves, abusive, without love,*
> *not possessing self-control, and lovers of pleasures*
> *rather than lovers of God.*
>
> —2 TIMOTHY 3:2-4

In the face of this duplicity I devised a plan, one used by many men far better than myself. I concluded that this world, my entire family, and God Himself would be better off if I just ended the problem, which of course was ME. I decided to end my life. There seemed to be no better solution to my dilemma. I convinced myself that God would understand, forgive, and make special allowances for my choice.

Dressed in one of Carol Ann's favorite outfits, I spent the entire day among women in various shopping malls; I even went to dinner at a well-known restaurant for my "last supper." I was desperate because either road I chose was filled with unbearable regret, pain, and anguish. It was nearing midnight when I parked my car in the large parking lot and walked several miles to the river's edge where I could be swept away. My heart railed at God. I never thought it would come to this. *All I wanted was to become the woman You should have made me.*

As I glanced up one last time at the brilliant moonlit sky, my soul suddenly cried out, *Lord, if there's another way out of this pain, show me now!* Tears flowed.

Then it happened. A sliver of light pierced the darkness of my soul. "There is freedom from this. Go and tell Mr. Maxes; tell him your secret." The voice was unmistakable.

Slowly, I backed up from the riverside and I spoke aloud. "I will give it one more try."

The Turning Point

The next evening I drove into our church parking lot and walked resolutely into Mr. Maxes's office. As a devoted follower of Christ and a trained counselor, Mr. Maxes made himself available to members of the church on certain evenings. On his desk I piled a stack of picture albums chronicling my secret life in living color. On top of the stack I placed the note of my riverside attempt. I looked at him directly and asked if there really is help for a person like me. I watched him intently as he opened the top album and glanced through its pages. He showed no hint of shock or disgust, no drawing back in horror. Most surprising of all, he didn't shrug his shoulders and parrot the words I'd heard so many times before. "Well, as far as I know there is no hope for change. You just need to begin to accept who you really are."

Instead I had heard him encourage me. "Yes, there is hope for change. Jesus left nothing outside of the cross. I am not saying it will happen overnight. I assure you that it will sometimes be very painful, but you won't be going it alone. We will enlist the help of others within the church to come alongside you and your wife. You don't have to fight this battle by yourselves any longer. Together, we can make it. Let's begin to find out what's at the bottom of this."

That visit marked the turning point in my life. "We're only as sick as our secrets," one psychologist had told me. I knew his words were true. Two decades of living a double life within the family of God were coming to an end. Discarding my secret identity was excruciatingly painful. At first I didn't know if I could emotionally survive without the cross-dressing. Eventually I could see that abandoning the old behavior and receiving Christ's healing for my damaged emotions was the best thing for me. Anything less would have been certain death.

I have come to deeply appreciate the words of John Michael Talbot:

> "Healer of my soul, keep me at evening, in the
> morning and at noon. Help me and safeguard me,
> for I am tired of straining and stumbling. Shield
> my soul from the snare of sin. Heal my soul."

The unconditional love and prayers of God's people have done more than I can express to bring about the restoration of my soul. Elizabeth Moberly is right in saying:

> "Prayer is at the heart of healing, and God's love is
> concerned in all aspects of the brokenness of our
> lives. We can offer Him all of our past as well as
> our present and future. This does not mean writing
> off the past, but opening it up to the healing love
> of Christ. The undoing and transformation of the
> effects of the past is one of our greatest needs."[7]

Today, as I share my thoughts with you, I can see fresh evidence of the changing seasons. One glimpse out of my office window

---

7 Elizabeth Moberly, *Homosexuality: A New Christian Ethic*, (Attic Press, 1983), 43.

reminds me that the leaves are once again turning into a brilliant red. My reflection in the windowpane is radically different from the day I sat in Dr. Nancy's office. It is no longer that of a stylish woman waiting for the receptionist's call. Now I see the man God had created me to be. I am at peace being Jerry.

Chapter 2

Understanding Napoleon

Transgender Dysphoria is a term that attempts to describe a condition in which individuals are at war with their primary gender assignment and basic sexual identity. It may be better defined in this way: *Transgender dysphoria is an incongruence that exists between the biological reality and the self-declared gender identity. Transgender* means *the crossing of (trans) gender lines.* In reality, crossing gender lines is impossible because gender is a part of the most fundamental makeup of a male or female, an essence not dependent upon hormones, or secondary sex characteristics. It is God-breathed.

Gender refers to the basic essence of who we are as human beings. It is a most sacred trust and responsibility. The Bible makes it clear from the beginning that God makes us male and female. In the design given by our Creator, our gender is not in question. It's written clearly in the basic genetic structure and chromosomes (XX or XY). At the moment of conception, gender is a "done deal." The chromosomes and other unique physiological formations are simply the compliant bodily response to the Divine assignment.

The Unalterable Reality

Gender is God's unalterable reality.

> "Invariably when a soul needs healing there will be an imbalance within of the masculine and the feminine. He or she is tipping the scales too far toward one extreme of the continuum."[8]

---

8 Payne, Leanne. *Crisis in Masculinity* (p. 87). Baker Publishing Group. Kindle Edition.

"Gender participates in the mystery of being itself. And in the anguish of the human person—stretched to whatever degree between being and nonbeing—his or her masculine or feminine identity and the balance with its polar opposite are always to be reckoned with."[9]

Brad Sargent writes in "Understanding Male Transvestism:"

"Gender refers to genetic sex (male or female), which is irreversibly fixed at the moment of conception by the pairing of the twenty-third chromosomes. Hence, gender is biologically determined. I think this is a very key scientific fact: gender is biologically determined, and there is nothing that can alter that. Identity, on the other hand, is environmentally or psychologically determined; a product of how one views the self. A male is always a male. A female is always a female. But a man can take on the appearance or the identity of a woman and a woman can take on the external appearance of a man. This is the process of identifying oneself with one sex or the other and it is typically completed within the first three or four years of life."[10]

Looking back, I found that true in my life. Certainly, by the time I was three-and-a-half years of age I was well on my way to either homosexuality or transgender confusion. I'm convinced I had repressed same-sex desires that never fully manifested or surfaced because of my own family's abhorrence to homosexual behavior.

---

9 Ibid, (p. 97)
10 Brad Sargent, "Understanding Male Transvestism," (1991), 10.

But in later years, I reasoned that if I could become a woman, then I could have a meaningful relationship with a man in order to get the love I so craved. I never really pictured myself as a man married to a man. But, in living in the attractive role of the woman, I could then truly be loved and affirmed. So, even though I never acted out those homosexual impulses, I certainly did entertain erotic fantasies about the enviable place of being affectionately cared for and embraced by a man, but only if it were in the role of Carol Ann. (Isn't it interesting that the very symbol for the word erotic, or Eros love is depicted as a serpent devouring its own tail?)

Male celebrities today claim to be expressing their "feminine side" when cross-dressing. However, the facts about gender are set in concrete. God has made us one particular gender, male or female. A young man may have feminine interests and temperament, or even go to the extreme of having sex-reassignment surgery (SRS), but two irrefutable facts remain: (1) God makes no mistakes, and (2) the surgeon's scalpel can only rearrange human skin; it cannot excise or heal the wounds of the human soul. You can change one's sexual identity by cosmetic surgery, but you cannot change a person's gender. That is permanently, inseparably, and very intentionally etched into one's being at conception.

Don't be Confused about Dysphoria

Dysphoria means "confusion, disorientation, or a general loss of equilibrium." Objectors would like to eliminate this technical medical definition, but it has remained intact so far.

Furthermore, Robert McGee identifies the outcome of damaged self-esteem:

> "The feeling of significance is crucial to man's emotional, spiritual, and social stability and is a driving element within the human spirit."[11]

When our sense of being is attacked, personal equilibrium is severely affected. So when people say that certain people have transgender dysphoria, they are trying to explain that these individuals are struggling to accept the male or female anatomical body they were given at birth. The result: Severe emotional dizzy spells (dysphoria). These individuals endlessly strive to bring resolution to their conflicting feelings by dressing in the attire of the opposite sex, trying to make their outsides match what they feel inside. It's a humanly devised way to momentarily or permanently make the outward sexual appearance match the confused, disoriented, inward longings of the heart. They are merely attempting to escape their God-assigned gender and sexual status in order to function within the sexual status of the opposite gender—that which the damaged soul has longed for all along.

The foundations of transgenderism are recorded in Isaiah 14 and Ezekiel 28, where Lucifer, a created archangel (along with Gabriel and Michael), became proud and lifted up because of his own beauty and corrupted his wisdom for the sake of his splendor. He profaned himself by the "many sins and dishonest trade" and enormous guilt (Ezekiel 28:17-18). This angel became corrupt because the iniquity-drive of self-will within his own heart compelled him to decide for himself what he deemed best. It was already quite plain

---

11 Robert B Shaw, Jr., *Created for Significance*, WestBow Press, 2013, p. 4.

what God's intent for him was to be. But he became puffed up and rebelled, no longer satisfied to keep his God-appointed place. The devil once was an angel, but he thought he knew better than God what his real purpose should be in the universe. (See Isaiah 14:12-16.) Some things never change.

When we elect to have physicians and surgeons rearrange skin-folds and remove body parts to attempt to bring our God-designed anatomy more in line with our depraved self-view, we are declaring our way to better than our Creator's way. We arrogantly boast, "You know, I'm just not content with my life the way God designed it. I'm going to have my sexual status changed, leave my family, break my covenant with my wife (or husband), and enter into a lifestyle that God did not prescribe for me—knowing full well that God loves me, understands, and will let me get away with it."

In response to that I ask a simple question: If the devil, who was once an angel of God, can take such a disgraceful fall, what makes us think we can follow his lead and be excused? We have a problem when the devilish inner compass of our un-renewed hearts compels us into overt rebellion against God's obvious intentions. This is succinctly addressed in the *Sexaholics Anonymous Handbook:*

> "The problem we all face is that of trying to tend our wounds by ourselves, looking in all the wrong places or to the wrong people for their input or remedy. Most of us have felt inadequate, unworthy of true love, very alone, and fearful. It seems that what we experience within seldom matches what we see portrayed in the lives of others.

"From the earliest age, we came to feel disconnected from our parents, peers, and even from ourselves. We tuned out of the real world through fantasy, masturbation, experimenting with cross-dressing, escaping into our false feminine world, and entertaining ourselves with even more escapades into more fantasy.

"We plugged in by consuming the pictures and the erotic images, and by pursuing the objects of our lust-filled fantasies. We lusted and wanted to be lusted after. We became true addicts. We entered into increasingly risky behavior to achieve more thrilling experiences.

"We bought it, we sold it, we traded it, and we gave it away. We have been addicted to the intrigue, the tease, and the forbidden. The only way we have known to be free of it was to do it! We cried with outstretched arms, 'Please connect with me and make me whole!' Lusting after the 'big fix', we gave away our power to others. This produced an inner emotional 'pool of pain' containing guilt, remorse, shame, self-contempt, loneliness, and emptiness— covered over by the phony exterior. In the process, we were driven inward, away from reality, away from true love, lost inside ourselves, with no one who genuinely understands. Our habitual return to the 'quick fix' has made true intimacy impossible.

"We could never know what true intimacy was about with another human being because we were chronically addicted to the fantasy, the unreal, and the imagined world of make believe. Our chief goal has been to go for the body chemistry, the magical connection that had the magical turn-on, which, of course, passed for true intimacy and true union with another human. Our fantasy life has corrupted what could have been real. Lust killed true love. First, we became addicted.

"We became severely handicapped by our pursuit of that which can never satisfy. We stole from others in order to fill up what we felt lacking in ourselves. We have conned ourselves over and over again, believing that the next encounter really would save us, make things better, when in reality we were really losing our very lives.

"If we're going to encounter reality and final reso-lution, we need to surrender ourselves again and again to the disciplined process of meeting with each other, admitting to others the true revelation of the true need of our hearts. Our cry has to turn from the self-consuming demand, 'Connect with me to make me whole!' Instead, we must face the truth we've run from and then turn to our Eternal Creator. Then the healing and transformation begins."[12]

---

12 *Sexaholics Anonymous Handbook*, (SA Publishers, 1989), 68.

Chapter 3

Come and Get Me, Dad

Because transgenders have suffered such a breakdown in their psychosocial development, they end up erotically idolizing (cannibalizing) the other sex, believing that being one of them would be the appropriate medicinal agent to cure the intense emotional pain.

When a man refuses to accept himself, his eyes are inherent masculinity. The son needs to be persuaded to leave his mother's nurturing presence.

> "Because the mother is present and accessible, the boys' most focused emotion says, "Let go of me, Mom!" But his more primal cry is rather, "Come and get me, Dad!"[13]

As Leanne Payne suggests:

> "The finest and most capable mother, try as she may, cannot repair the gap an absent or emotionally remote father leaves on the young teenager. She simply cannot affirm a son or daughter in the way a whole father can. This is one of the awful tragedies of divorce and broken homes. There is seldom a father substitute who is both capable and willing to affirm the struggling adolescent boy or girl."[14]

---

13 Gorden Dalbey, *Father & Son*, (Thomas Nelson, 92), 40
14 Payne, Leanne. *The Broken Image* (pp. 39-40). Baker Publishing Group. Kindle Edition.

Further, it's abundantly clear from the personal experience of so many, that a boy's overbonding with the mother, therefore, reflects a weak or an absent father . . . leaving an awful, gaping wound in his own masculine soul from not having been called out by his own father into the company of men.

Mom's Emotional Apron Strings

One primary commonality is that male transgenders have never effectively detached from Mom's emotional apron strings. It's not that she was necessarily a smothering kind of influence; perhaps her greatest sin is that she was simply the more available and affirming, or more desirable of the two parents.

Joseph Nicolosi stresses:

> "The father has to be a strong and attractive enough parent to induce the son to leave the comfortable relationship and original identification with mother."[15]

Billie, a post-operative male-to-female transgender, honestly related:

> "My hatred for being a man became the turning point for my becoming a transgender, although it's not the only reason. If I did not hate to be a man, I would still be one. When standing naked in front of a mirror, I hated my male organs, which my therapist affirmed as a real piece of evidence that proved I was truly a transgender.

---

15 Joseph Nicolosi, *Reparative Therapy of Male Homosexuality*, (Jason Aronson, 1991).

As we absorb estrogen, our emotions do change and many times we find men becoming more attractive to us, but while we are in that male state, before hormone therapy, many of us did indeed hate men. This hatred is often resolved by taking female hormones. But the underlying reason I was a transgenders was from my hatred for men, and the hatred for own body, as well as the role I have to play as a man."

Female-to-Male Transgenderism

The opposite is true with the female. Elaine's account is a prime example as she relates the severe emotional abuse at the hand of her oldest brother. Her story is similar to many desiring to be the opposite sex. Elaine writes:

"I trusted my brother completely, and he told me to eat three garden worms if I wanted to be like him. He promised me that a meal of worms would change me into a boy. I dug up the garden and finally found three worms and swallowed them whole! It was a most unpleasant experience, but I overcame all the discomfort of imagining the worms crawling around in my stomach, with the extreme hope of being changed from this dreaded, weak, unwanted state of being a girl to the glorious state of being a boy."

Marti's Story

Marti, a dear friend, recounts his ongoing battle with his gender identity, even after a period of active recovery:

"Most days aren't hard for me anymore. But some days are harder than others, and this was one of them. This past Tuesday, I was working in a part of town where I used to do a lot of acting out, and I was having a rough time controlling my mind. Right around the corner was one of the dress shops I used to go to. The ladies there knew me and liked me. I was nobody special to them, just another sissy guy wearing a dress, which is not that uncommon here. But they accepted and liked me.

"The place drew me that day like a magnet, but I did not give in. I just kept right on working, but I was really on edge. Then this really pretty girl walked by. She was totally feminine. She had a real talent for walking down the street. She could make a career out of just walking if she wanted to. Three of us men turned our heads as she passed. She gave a quick look over her shoulder to make sure everyone was looking at her. Of course, we all were! That was when I lost it! I started thinking, 'Look at the way she turns all of these men's heads as she walks by. I want to do that. I'm missing out on all the fun in life.' Then another lie popped into my head, 'You haven't done enough yet, Marti! Why don't you go back; do all the things you've never done, but dreamed about. Then you can quit. You've only lived out about half of your dreams. You won't be young forever, you know. Don't waste your time fighting against feelings, fighting against yourself. Get out and start having fun again! If you really want to serve God, you can do that later! Besides, think of how much more valuable your testimony will be after having been there and done that.

"My mind ran wild. By the time I returned home from work, I had no more resistance. Forget about all the progress I'd made the past year and how far I'd come in my recovery from this diseased and twisted way of thinking. I was going back!

"While I was taking a shower, getting ready to go out, God gently intervened. He gave me a picture, clear and vivid. The picture, which lasted a very short time, spoke volumes to my heart. I saw an old man, about 150 years old. He was very frail and hunched over, standing outside, peering in through an open doorway.

"He didn't want anyone to see him, so he hid himself, only sticking his head around the doorway. The expression on his face was similar to that of a homeless man, hopeless and lost. But there was more to it than that. The defining feature of his face was the deep, deep sorrow that seemed to reach down to his very bones.

"I could actually feel his heaviness and sorrow heave within my own body. He was looking at a bunch of people seated around a long, rectangular table, eating and laughing and truly enjoying life. The house was filled with joy. There was no reason the old man could not go through the door, take a seat at the table and join them. He just looked through the doorway for a while, his sorrow increasing. Then he moved on. He had made a life of choosing misery over joy, isolation over fellowship, sorrow over blessings, and his own way over God's way, That was it! That was the whole picture. That was when I understood that I'd be the old man if I returned to my old ways. God had given me a gentle reminder of what I was really going back to and what I was about to leave behind. I was not going back to a life of fun-filled dreams somehow magically realized. I was not going back to reality, but to mere fantasy, a world of ribbon and lace that was not mine to have. I was going back to loneliness and shame. I was going back to separation from the ones I loved, back to slavery and thoughts of suicide as the only remaining means of escape.

"Contrary to my old beliefs, crossing gender lines is not about finding my true self and releasing the real me; it's about losing my true self. It is not about growing and becoming. It's about shrinking and ultimately disappearing.

It's about deceiving and being deceived. It's all about losing. God is giving me a new identity now. The new me is cleaned up and evidencing degrees of holiness because He has made me that way. I can't believe I ever thought, even for a moment, of ever going back to that so-called life. I can only plead temporary insanity! I never felt as though I had a choice before. But now I know that I do. Unlike the old man in the picture, I'm choosing life and joy and God's way. He is the one who made me and has removed the fictitious illusion of femininity, which only left me with such horrid emptiness. He's faithfully doing His work in me, patiently molding me and making me into what He wanted from the start."

An Instructive word on this is written by the Apostle James. Listen to his perspective:

"Where do you think all these appalling wars and quarrels come from? Do you think they just happen? Think again. They come about because you want your own way, and fight for it deep inside yourselves. You lust for what you don't have and are willing to kill to get it. You want what is not yours and will risk violence to get your hand on it.

"You wouldn't think of just asking God for it, would you? And why not? Because you know you would be asking what you have no right too. You are spoiled children, each wanting your own way.

You are cheating on God. If all you want is your own way, flirting with the world every chance you get, you end up enemies of God and His way. And do you suppose God doesn't care? The proverb has it that 'he's a fiercely jealous lover' and what He gives in love is far better than anything else you will find. It's common knowledge that God goes against the willful proud; God gives grace to the willing humble. So let God work His will in you. Yell aloud no to the devil and watch him scamper Say a quiet yes to God and he will be there in no time. Quit dabbling in sin. Purify your inner life. Quit playing the field. Hit bottom, and cry your eyes out. The fun and games are over. Get serious, really serious. Get down on your knees before the Master; it's the only way you'll get on your feet (James 4:1-10, The Message)."

About Napoleon

What would you do if you were engaged in a military conflict and your commanding officer entered your barracks dressed as Napoleon Bonaparte? (And it isn't Halloween!) To make matters worse, he approaches you, claiming to be the *real* Napoleon? If you protest, he demands that you consider his claim and behavior as nothing out of the ordinary. He may even justify his behavior, saying, "This is who I was always meant to be. You just have to accept me the way I am. This is the real me."

I hope you would get him help before the day's end. Otherwise, things could be disastrous for all concerned. That's what's going on today. Folks dress up, pretending to be someone they're not, then ask others (maybe a wife, mother, father, or other family members) to accept them "as is"—and all is supposed to be normal. They're even asking or demanding the family of God accept their "new creation" without protest.

One husband and father wrote to his doctor, "Sure, I know that I look like a man, but I've always felt like a woman on the inside, and I'm pretty sure that I have a female brain. And I think I would like 38C breast implants, if that's all right with you. You can help me fulfill my lifelong dream."

The doctor's response essentially was, "Step right this way into surgical suite A."

The real question is this: **Why is the medical community so completely accepting of Sex Reassignment Surgery (SRS) as the only truly effective treatment for people with transgender issues?** Could it be due to their mistaken belief that if they lack a cure, then all other approaches to healing are a hopeless waste of time? It would seem that this is the case. Because if doctors reason that inward peace within a person's gender is beyond their realm of expertise, then the only compassionate, humanitarian recourse is to do the surgery and hormonal replacement to prevent the tormented patient from either going insane or committing suicide.

Recovery programs for other addictions (AA, GA, SA, and Al Anon) don't follow this philosophy. The method followed in each of these programs is to break down the denial and uncover the root issues that are causing the person to find such destructive and mutilating ways to escape the hard realities. Is it true compassion to assist someone in denying reality—and the restorative grace and power of our Lord and Savior, Jesus Christ?

Time for Honesty

If a Christian man becomes honest with himself, he will have to admit that he's in the wrong and at cross-purposes with the Lord's intention for his life when he embraces the world's solution to gender confusion, which is sex-reassignment surgery. The sin is not found merely in the cross-dressing; that's simply the indicator of a far more serious malady—sin of the rebellious heart.

At its core, the real issue is the age-old sin described in Isaiah 53:6: "We all, like sheep, have gone astray, each of us has turned to our own way."

Psalm 14:12 (KJV) puts it this way: "There is a way that appears to be right but in the end it leads to death." Now is an intense time for me to examine myself in light of what I am and am becoming.

Psalm 51:6 says, "You desired faithfulness even in the womb; you taught me wisdom in that secret place."

This is what I truly want! But I find that my heart is deceptive. On the one hand I think I'm doing the right thing, but the fruit of what I'm doing shows otherwise. I won't be one to justify myself or twist the Scriptures to fit my position.

What is the fruit of my actions? Does it please God or edify and build up my brothers and sisters in Christ? Do my actions glorify God to the world? First Corinthians 6:20 proclaims that we are bought with a price and are no longer our own, and that we are to glorify God in our body and spirit, both of which belong to God.

So far, I've hurt the woman I love the very most—and have lost my marriage covenant. I would honestly say that the fruit I've borne so far is not good. Yet I justify it because I say, "I'm being true to my female self."

Association

Most transgender people circulate almost exclusively in the TG community, and the TG community has strong ties to the gay and lesbian community. I think the Scriptures are abundantly clear on this one. Romans 1 & 2, along with 1 Corinthians 6:9, reveal God's view on homosexuality. I honestly have never felt comfortable with this issue, because I know the Bible too well. I know from experience that I'm not gay. I have asked the Lord to forgive me of these shameful acts, the kinds that are never admitted to in public because they're so lurid and sensual. I have played the TG/Gay/Lesbian club scene and found that most there are interested in one thing: sex. For me this is a major turn off and huge problem. No good associations here.

Other-Centered or Self-Centered?

One man said:

> "Lately I've found myself consumed with my false-feminine persona, Harriet. I'm constantly thinking of how to improve my appearance and be her on a full-time basis. I'm consumed with dressing, walking, talking, acting, breathing, and smelling like a woman. My main focus is, 'Am I passing or not?'"

By nature, we should not be thinking about our gender. Our gender should be as natural as our breathing. God's way is for us to be other-centered, and that means Christ-centered. We're told to "seek first his kingdom and his righteousness" (Matthew 6:33) and to "in humility value others above yourselves" (Philippians 2:3). It seems easier, and perhaps more profitable to some who stand to directly to benefit from the revenue, to just accept the neurotic behavior and demands of Napoleon.

Of course those who love Napoleon want to remain in relationship with him, but if they're willing to resist the temptation to seek peace at any price, they might lovingly clasp his elbow, saying, "Careful there, my dear friend, your equilibrium's a bit off. Let's get someone to help you."

The Church's Confession

Rev. Ed Flook confessed to those who have been wounded:

> "We have not been authentic. We have not had much to offer you to help you find freedom in Christ. We have practiced, and by example taught, an anemic variety of Christianity, holding to a form of godliness, but denying the power thereof. We have failed to make disciples. We have been so driven by our need to appear successful that we have focused on activities that will produce quick results. We have avoided engagement with 'messy' people who are coming out of patterns that may take a lifetime to heal. I confess on behalf of the church that: We have settled for a weak imitation

of real Christianity. For this reason we have often had little to offer to those who needed to find God's power to break free of sin. We have failed to provide a place for those coming out of these conditions, either in our churches or in our hearts. When you have needed a healed, whole, and loving church family to return to in the Lord, we have not been there for you. In many cases, we have given the impression that there is no place for you to go. Please forgive us and please come home to the church. You are part of us: it's your birthright, and we need you."[16]

---

16 Ed Flook, "A Pastor's Confession to the Church," Exodus International newsletter, 1991).

Chapter 4

What Caused This Confusion?

What creates such confusion and torment in the first place? Where did the false-feminine Carol Ann originate? How did I end up at the river's edge, only a breath away from plummeting into eternity? What happens to the human psyche to bring one to such a state of mind? What can bring resolution to such deeply entrenched forms of sexual/gender-identity confusion? Is it possible for the transgender person to ever be truly satisfied with his/her gender?

There are no easy answers, but there are answers. We have to dig deep to find them, way down to the roots. If you want freedom, you have to pursue it, and it will take perseverance and stubbornness to achieve lasting peace. As Dutch Sheets explains:

> "Stubbornness is one of the most important spiritual attributes of the Christian life".

Charles Spurgeon said,

> "By perseverance the snail reached the ark."

A lack of endurance is one of the greatest causes of defeat. *In the Grip of Grace* puts it this way:

> "We don't wait well. We are into micro-waving God; while He is, on the other hand, usually into marinating."[17]

---

17 Max Lucado, *In the Grip of Grace*, (Word, 1996), 24.

"I don't feel that I have made any progress at all with this. I have given in to cross-dressing for so long that I don't know what I'd ever do without it. Is it really possible for me to ever be 'normal,' with a regular sex drive? I don't ever remember being normal, and I'm really having a problem perceiving of myself that way. Can God put something in me that had never existed before? If I get rid of this aspect of my life, what in the world would there be to replace it?"

A dear friend shares:

> "I had completed my journal for the day, writing about my determination to fully embrace the feminine identity for which I longed my entire life. I had recorded my 'last will and testament,' settling on my detailed plan to leave my beloved wife and children for the fulfillment of my life-long dream. I wrote:

> "I can't escape the relentless thoughts and desires of my heart to fulfill the long-awaited dream. I'm no longer just a mere "dreamer' but am now pursing headlong what my heart has wanted all these years. I will not allow anything to stop me. I cannot let others' views deter me from reaching my true destiny. It's the only thing that gives me purpose for living. It's my life, my true love. All that would detain me must get out of my way. I want to believe that you, God, are with me in this venture. But even if you aren't,

*I say to you as well, 'Get out of my way!' I can
and will do nothing other than this. I will be a
woman, no matter the cost. Nothing or no one
will stop me."*

I now read this and shudder, realizing the arrogant rebellion and
irrational thinking behind it. I still shake my head at what happened
upon closing the journal. God simply withdrew the conscious sense
of His Presence. In some ways it paralleled what C.S. Lewis states in
his powerful book *The Great Divorce*:

> "There are only two kinds of people in the end:
> those who say to God, 'Thy will be done' and those
> to whom God says in the end, 'Thy will be done.'"[18]

It is because of our heart's disposition that occasionally the sense of
His presence seems to be withdrawn. In our rebellion, we suppress
the raw truth in the hope that somehow our futile, dark reasoning,
inspired by the iniquity of our own twisted heart, will prevail. But
God's love persists in hating that which deters us from intimacy with
Him. His white-hot anger at our hearts' preoccupations with evil is
engulfed by His grace. Nevertheless, we so carelessly sell our soul
for the bowl of instant gratification the incomprehensible tradeoff
of His eternal presence for the fantasy of the moment. Fantasies
become reality.

Harry Schaumburg understands the dynamic of sinful sexual behavior and unmasks it in his masterful work, *False Intimacy*:

---

18 C.S. Lewis, *The Great Divorce*, (MacMillan, 1971), 72.

> "Sinful behaviors do provide a certain level of fulfillment or they would never be tempting. They offer a momentary escape or the illusion of relief. But following our sinful desires always suppresses the truth of who God is and what He says about us in the Bible."[19]

We can choose to worship other things in His place. The central issue is idolatry. The truth about God is suppressed by our wickedness (see Romans 1:18). As we honor God, we will move to honor others. As we dishonor God, we dishonor ourselves and others.

Three times in the opening chapter of his letter to the Romans, Paul uses the expression "God gave them over." When we don't honor God, God also responds. When we sin in our hearts toward Him, refusing to be dependent upon Him, He gives us over to the control of the darkness of our hearts, which creates deeper darkness. He gives us over to our own cravings, allowing us to be controlled, literally, by those desires. Therefore, moral perversion is the result of our desires. We demand and choose to regulate our loves rather than honoring and obeying God. We've lost the ability to regulate our desires.

In *The Problem of Pain,* C.S. Lewis states that people will

> "enjoy forever the horrible freedom they have demanded, and are therefore self-enslaved . . . "[20]

---

19 Harry Schaumburg, *False Intimacy,* (NavPress, 1996), 24.
20 C.S. Lewis, Joyful Christian, (Scribner, 1996), p. 226.

Our Creator has what Max Lucado refers to as:

> "Call it holy hostility; righteous hatred of wrong, a divine disgust at the evil that destroys his children. The question is not, 'How dare a loving God be angry?' but rather, 'How could a loving God feel anything less?'"[21]

Venus Envy

Envy is one of the main issues in the transgender lifestyle. Usually by puberty this envy of the feminine is deeply tugging at the thoughts and emotions of a gender-confused boy. The normal joys of childhood are stolen by the incessant reminders of his inadequacies and his missing out on what seems to be the most fun—all fueled by envy.

When a little boy should be praying for a new Tonka truck, he earnestly prays to wake up in the morning as a girl. Envy coupled with jealousy and accompanying idealistic fantasies, gives rise to unrealistic notions that being a female is easier, more advantageous, and more exciting! It holds out the prospect of finally (or again) experiencing the protective love, security, and nurturing comfort of one's own memories of mother, a love terribly craved.

One devout feminist said it so well:

> "Cross-dressing is really the opposite of what has happened in the feminist movement. The feminist movement was all about needing to share in the male experience, to get out of the bedrooms

---

21 Max Lucado, Pearls from the Prophets, (Xulon Press, 2008), p. 350.

and into the boardrooms. But meanwhile men have suffered from Venus envy. There is a deep need in men to feel soft, to be glamorous, to do housework."[22]

Cross dressing is not just an innocent act. It's the result of many deep-seated, perceived or real, rejections and the incredible envy of girls who were accepted, loved, and cared for—those who got away with things and seemingly had life better just because they wore dresses.

Katherine, the sister of a post-operative male-to-female transgender wrote:

> "I realized that his lifetime struggle had not
> been to become something or someone, but to
> destroy something. It seemed to me that Phil
> was shaking his fist at God, saying, 'I hate the
> way you made me, and, see, I did something
> about it.'

Transgenders who are considering surgery eventually become convinced that the discomfort in having to live out what they consider a lie that "God made me a man" is more incomprehensible than proceeding with sexual-reassignment surgery.

They realize that the decision to have their sexual identity surgically altered is filled with many difficulties and painful events (such as risking the loss of job, friends, and family), but they become willing to pay the price. Remaining in their present sexual identity becomes entirely unthinkable. Their mental obsession conquers more ground

---

22 Veronica Vera, "Boys Will be Girls," (*Bazaar Magazine*, October 1994), 24.

daily, leading to the point of absolute despair in having to face another day living as a man.

Ultimate Blame Shifting: It's God's Fault

One certain giveaway that the enemy has occupied the heart and soul of the practicing transgender is by the lies he's believed (his own reality)—and what he now proclaims as truth. One such false assertion is that God's genetic engineering somehow got messed up, that in fact the transgender person is really a freak of nature, a member of the opposite sex trapped mercilessly in the wrong body. The designer is at fault! Adam, the first man who refused to take responsibility for his own actions, also shifted the blame to God in the Garden of Eden, saying it's "The woman you put here with me" (Genesis 3:12). That line sounded good, and many use it even today. Some things never change. Adam's victim mentality prevails today in the genetic theories. The natural conclusion is that when a person is "victimized" by a birth "mistake," it's foolish not to do something to correct the mistake. Many attest by their decisions to have surgery that they can no longer tolerate assuming the role of that which has become to them a cosmic joke.

Many feel their brain physiology and chemistry are truly that of the opposite gender. The reason for this is relatively obvious: They have spent so much time fantasizing about being a legally recognized member of the opposite sex that they begin to see themselves that way. They conclude that their brain must have been "wired" that way by insufficient testosterone levels while in-utero, or something akin to that. And in one sense they're right.

Transgenders are wired differently, but the cause does not conform to politically correct thought. It is chiefly the result of the neuro-chemical pathways that have created superhighways in the brain structure by their obsessive-compulsive thoughts, fantasies, and behaviors. Fleshly indulgences create those kinds of addictive adrenaline rushes in more conditions than just in transgenderism. Many are learning to successfully recite the convincing and readily accepted lines of the transgender agenda. They talk incessantly about their unfortunate fate of suffering the results of a chromosomal mix up, attesting that blood studies would clearly indicate that they are truly a woman trapped in a man's body or vice a versa.

Real problems have resulted from recent disclosures by geneticists, who are themselves disproving the validity of the bogus, so-called scientific studies to support the theory of a genetic predisposition toward homosexuality and transgenderism. Since those studies have failed to truly prove anything conclusive, the current fad is to blame the gender mix up on an insufficient flow of sex-producing hormones when the embryo is still being formed in the mother's womb.

> "We will reach for anything that will somehow validate the way we want to live, and in the process we become self-deceived."[23]

All attempts are made to officially validate their propositions and gain the sympathy of the naïve and unsuspecting culture. As with Napoleon, we really want you to believe that one was meant to be Napoleon, so that you will be persuaded that we are only doing what "Mother Nature" was trying to do all the while anyway. The transgender person does not want to lose your love or acceptance.

---

23 M. Scott Peck, *People of the Lie: The Hope for Healing Human Evil*, (Touchstone, 1998).

He hopes to find it in his idealized new self. We simply want "the best" of both worlds. What an absolute heaven on earth we think it would be if we could live out our fantasy with all previous human relationships left intact.

Chapter 5

The Failure of the "Fix"

From my present vantage point, I now realize how self-absorbed I became as an active transgender. Transgenders become locked into an extreme form of self-absorption because of the accumulated rejection, abandonment, ridicule, shame, secrets, psychological splitting (Borderline Personality Disorder), guilt, and shame.

As Pat, a high-profile business executive recently said to me:

> "I've grown tired of trying to measure up to the
> world's expectations of me as a man. It's just
> too hard. I want to stay at home, clean house,
> read women's magazines, go shopping, tend to
> my garden, and feel good about life."

Borderline Personality Disorder

It's vital that we understand the depth of psychological splitting that occurs. I've often referred to myself as emotionally ill, and it's true. We transgenders obviously suffer from what professionals call "Borderline Personality Disorder" (among other emotional disorders), as professionals defined it so clearly in the DSM-IV (Diagnostic and Statistical Manual of Mental Disorders) compiled by the American Psychiatric Association.

As explained in the DSM-IV, Borderline Personality Disorder is an obtrusive and pervasive pattern of emotional instability, especially in the context of interpersonal relationships and one's self-image. It severely affects the child at an early chronological onset, evidenced by marked impulsiveness beginning by early adulthood and present in a variety of contexts, as indicated by five (or more) of the following:

- Frantic efforts to avoid real or imagined abandonment

- A pattern of unstable and intense interpersonal relationships characterized by alternation between extremes of idealization and devolution

- Identity disturbance: markedly and persistently unstable self-image or sense of self

- Impulsiveness in spending, sex, substance abuse, or binges

- Recurrent suicidal behavior, gestures, threats, or self-mutilating behavior

- Affective instability due to a marked reactivity of mood (e.g., intense episodic dysphoria, irritability, or anxiety usually lasting a few hours and only rarely more than a few days)

- Chronic feelings of emptiness

- Inappropriate, intense anger or difficulty controlling anger

- Transient, stress-related paranoid ideation or severe dissociative symptoms

It is further noted that Borderline Personality Disorders (BPD) occur specifically in those afflicted by Gender Identity Disorder, Obsessive-Compulsive Disorders, Mood Disorders, Panic Attack Disorders, Multiple Personality Disorders, and substance abuse to name a few. Indirectly, over 75 percent of those struggling with Borderline Personality Disorder (BPD) have been sexually abused.[24]

------

24 Diagnostic & Statistical Manual III-R, "Bipolar Disorders," (American Psychiatric Association), 25.

Line upon Line, Brick upon Brick

Entering into transgender sex-change surgery is not just a one-time decision. It's the result of myriad insufferable choices and experiences in the trenches of a bloody war. Lies have been mercilessly hurtled into the very heart of young children, causing them to believe they would have been better off as a member the opposite gender. By the time the hormones begin to do their work of forming secondary sex characteristics, the emotional life of the child has already been mortally wounded.

Listen to Tracy's account of his painful childhood experiences and see if you can discern what brought him such discomfort with his gender identity:

> "My distortion of men was highly influenced by my early adolescent experiences. Many of us who are male-to-female transgenders have faced a certain amount of abuse at the hands of our male classmates. I was beaten frequently, thrown down a flight of stairs (twice), called every conceivable name, kicked, punched, sexually assaulted, and raped. While nothing my abusers did can be excused, it can be understood. Adolescence is the time when we establish our gender roles. It's a time of testing and exaggerating those roles. When one of us who did not fit the gender role stereotype came along, it presented a challenge that, developmentally, most of our male peers were unable to process. (Why should we expect them

to have been any more successful at processing this information then we were?) Most of our male peers just avoided us not sure how to deal with who we were. By the time the individual becomes an adult, he has little strength left to ward off the further attacks against his will. The transgender is not evil; he's just worn out by the lies, rejections, shame, and the all-too-frequent assaults. He finally gives up, yields to the lies that he has finally come to embrace as truth."

Peter Marshall, in his famous sermon "Our Friend, the Enemy," hit the target when he said:

"For any of us . . . the temptation is to put ourselves first, at the center of life, to play at being God. 'I want what I want! My will over God's will.' The human will is always free. God will force no man to obey Him, nor will He shield any from temptation. The sin is not in being tempted but in yielding. The temptation is always to purchase popularity by joining the crowd around the bargain counters of hell, when in exchange of an irrecoverable, fragile, precious thing—purity—the devil will offer cheap, glittering baubles with his hooks that are baited."[25]

---

25 Catherine Marshall, *The Best of Peter Marshall*, (Chosen Books, 1993), 246-47.

Abandoning the Search for the True Masculine

Unlike the homosexual who searches for another male to help complete him, the transgender eventually abandons the expedition for this lost manhood. He aborts the mission and hopes to start over again, even if it means living the rest of his life as a captive. Tired of living a double life, he finally surrenders to the overpowering desires that have so long raged within him. He begins his flight toward women with a passionate zeal, determined not to let anything or anyone deter him from reaching his goal. There is an insidious underlying anger at God, which manifests in a growing distrust, coldness, and resistance to God's expectations of him. The result: He becomes imprisoned in selfishness, hate and bitterness, with deception ever standing guard against any infusions of the truth.

Listen to the experience of Luke:

> "My divorce with my wife was finalized two months ago. She does not want to talk to me and would rather consider me dead. My dad totally disowns me and does not even want to talk to me. My mom is okay with me either way. She's the only one who loves me unconditionally. I really miss church. I have an appointment with a pastor of a church that I think I will like.
>
> "They are conservative, which created certain problems in and of itself. I consider myself conservative, but I know they will have a problem with what I have done. No one seems to understand that all I want to do is live

a quiet life as a woman. I want to be celibate because I hate male sex urges and anything to do with sexual activity. I know I'll suffer terrible loneliness the rest of my life.

"I firmly believe that the Bible condemns homosexuality. But, to be very honest, no one has been able to give me sufficient biblical grounds for not going forward with the surgery. I know that all my friends and fellow Christians will never accept me as a female, but I've come to firmly believe that God is more interested with the heart than outward appearance.

"I'm far more comfortable living as a woman. I feel whole and happy for the first time in my life. I am being real and honest at long last. What you now see is what you now get. This is the hardest thing I have had to do in my life, but I know that after the transition I'll be the happiest I've ever been. It's worth everything to do this. I leave the judgment to God. I know One day I'll have to answer to God for my actions, but it's worth it."

Danielle relates:

"My dad and I never got along. He was an abusive drunk to me and my mom. Mom protected me as best she could from his rage, but when he beat her, I hated him so, and I took sides with her. But the greatest hatred I have of all is not my hatred for Dad, but for God!

> He was the one who gave me such a father. If
> I could get even with God for that faulty plan,
> I would! In fact, I think I have, in part, by having
> my sex status altered, and removing myself
> from the family altogether and starting a life of
> my own design."

Paul clearly describes this condition in Romans 6:16: "Don't you know that when you offer yourselves to someone to obey him as slaves, you are slaves to the one you obey." Or, as *The Message* puts it, "There are some acts of so-called freedom that destroy freedom. Offer yourselves to sin, for instance, and it is your last free act."

The post-operative transgender will always be forced into living out a sexual/gender identity that can at best only be assumed. He will never become an authentic woman. The surgeon's scalpels can only accomplish the rearrangement or amputation of skin and underlying tissue. Surgery has no access to the ruptured heart, no way to stop the steady hemorrhaging in the depths of the soul.

Listen to the comments of Stephen, a post-operative transgender of twenty-one years:

> "When I took my first bath following the surgery,
> I looked down and saw the work that the
> surgeon had done. I said to myself, 'It's done!
> Everything is right now.' But nothing was really
> right. It did not cure me or take the pain inside
> my heart."

After the New Wears Off

When surgical alteration is accomplished, the postoperative trans-gender is understandably euphoric—at the beginning. He feels as if he's finally accomplished his mission, his reason for living. Now that he's accepted by others as a woman, he feels he has finally "arrived." This honeymoon stage may be prolonged, but sooner or later he must reckon with his delusion. Sadly, he ultimately discovers that his idealized dream was only an illusion. His efforts to take matters into his own hands will eventually prove to be unsatisfactory.

As one dear friend put it:

> "My life as a boring male has now been replaced
> by a life as a boring pseudo-female."

The painful insight comes when the transgender finally realizes that the great lengths to which he has gone were actually attempts to compete childhood's unfinished task of bonding with Mom—or a refusal to be separated from her—not to mention the sense of failure in never being able to receive Daddy's love and acceptance.

If the weary comrade seeks professional help, he will most usually be further disillusioned and devastated, since modernists have nothing to offer in the way of genuine help. If, however, the person were to become actively engaged in a serious soul-searching mission, and would honestly relate his discoveries, there would be a final admission that he has gone over the edge.

As a famous transgender, Rupal, confessed on national television:

> "Reality and I parted company a long, long time ago!"

Suicide is all too common when reality dawns. Other forms of medicinal relief—alcoholism, substance abuse, pornography, and exhibitionism through cultural art forms—are then routinely sought in order to anaesthetize the inner pain. Erotic, lustful activities simply take over. The reprobate mind sets up like concrete.

I recently spoke with a sixty-year-old man whose fulfilled dreams were only a few weeks old. He had successfully attained legal status as a woman, but was sobbing on the other end of the phone:

> "I've made the biggest mistake of my entire life!
> I'm still not able to get my dad's love. At his
> eighty-fifth-birthday celebration Dad announced
> that he was cutting me completely out of his
> inheritance because I was such a disgrace."

Why isn't the surgical procedure the panacea? Because boys will always be boys and girls will always be girls. As much as we may try (and God knows we do) we will always be our intended God-given gender.

As C.S. Lewis states:

> "The sexual identity of maleness can be escaped,
> for it really exists only on the biological level; but
> assigned gender is something from which none of
> us can escape—for gender is a reality more funda-
> mental than sexual identity."[26]

The insidious lies that postoperative transgenders must force upon those they want to mutually love are many. Self-deception turns

---

26 C.S. Lewis, *That Hideous Strength*, (Collier, 1962), 315.

into doing and saying whatever is necessary to convince others that what they have done is really okay, blessed of God, their true destiny.

A.W. Tozer, in his masterpiece, *Man: The Dwelling Place of God*, says:

> "Of all the forms of deception . . . self-deception is the most deadly, and of the all deceived persons, the self-deceived are the least likely to discover the fraud. The reason for this is simple. When a man is deceived by another he is deceived against his will. He is contending against an adversary and is temporarily the victim of another's guile. Since he expects his foe to take advantage of him he is watchful and quick to suspect trickery. Under such circumstance it is possible to be deceived sometimes and for a short while, but because the victim is resisting he may break out of the trap and escape before too long. With the self-deceived it is quite different. He is his own enemy and is working a fraud upon himself. He wants to believe the lie and is psychologically conditioned to do so. He does not resist the deceit but collaborates with it against himself. There is no struggle, because the victim surrenders before the fight begins. He enjoys being deceived."[27]

---

27 A.W. Tozer, *Man, The Dwelling Place of God*, (Christian Publications, 1966), 88-91.

Female Transgenderism: Personal Experiences

Let's take just a moment to look at the flip side of the coin. Many women suffer from this gender-identity disorder, too. It's typically easier for them to pass in public, because male hormones perform extraordinary physical changes in them. Testosterone produces muscles where girls don't normally have them. Male pattern baldness often occurs, along with a show of facial hair. Following a radical mastectomy, the transformed woman has a comparatively easy task in being accepted as a man. She might be perceived as a rather effeminate man, but few pick up on the masquerade.

Tamara, a recently divorced woman wrote:

> "I'm writing to you to ask questions about someone I love, a female who now lives as a male. When I first met this person, I tried to understand what was going on. I didn't know that he was really a female (post-operative). I found myself attracted to him and eventually fell in love. We've even talked about eventually getting married. There are so many problems with this. For example, he does not have male parts. And in order for his birth certificate to be changed, he's going to have a hysterectomy, which just does not make sense.
>
> "I've tried to push those thoughts aside and entertain myself with the fantasy of getting married. Steve is a wonderful person. I've seen pictures of him as a girl. He told me that throughout his life he'd felt that he really was a

boy. I've repeatedly told him that I thought he needs help, but I don't know what kind of help.

"On one hand, he's been the best man I have ever known; he treats me like a queen. On the other hand, his body is like mine, and I don't see that we would really 'fit' as God intends."

One of my close allies, Therese, a female-to-male transgender relates:

"It was too painful to be rejected, and my convincing male appearance fooled everyone. From a very early age, I was confused about my sexual identity and who I wanted to be. Even before entering kindergarten, I remember pretending to ride my tricycle to my imaginary girlfriend's house. But I could not tell anyone about her. An even deeper secret was my strong desire to actually become a little boy myself.

"Family life was dysfunctional. My dad was emotionally and verbally abusive. He didn't seem to know how to hug or say 'I love you'. In his jealousy, he accused mom of affairs that did not happen. Mom, on the other hand, was always seeking nurturing from me. I soon learned that for her to love me, it would cost me a lot.

"My older brother sexually abused me and I felt I had no one to talk to. I was already emotionally detached, but the abuse gave more reason to leave it that way. The desire to become a boy burned even greater. At the age of twelve, I became friends with a neighbor boy. We hung out a lot together and became inseparable.

"One day I confided in him my desire to become a man. He became very excited and said, 'Now we can become brothers.' With this acceptance, I began to dress as a boy, and he always covered for me. As we got older, we went to different schools. This worked to my advantage—I could go to his school dances as a boy. That's where I met my first girlfriend and began to live a double life. I moved out of the house at sixteen and began to live as a man at nineteen. I initiated male hormone therapy and was very excited. I remember thinking, *Now I'm free, now I'm complete*.

"I've changed my name to Tom."

A Parent's Influence

How important is the influence of each parent to the overall health of a developing child?

Molly, a female-to-male transgender wrote:

"I really believed that somehow my parents' divorce was my fault, that if I'd been the son my father wanted, he would not have left. I knew at a very young age that the only name chosen prior to my birth had been a boy's name."

In his book *Eros Redeemed*, John White states:

> "Our gender identity has to do with our sense or perception of our being manly or womanly, masculine or feminine. The influence is that gender identity has nothing to do with biology or what is physically true, but, rather what we think about ourselves as men and women."[28]

John Freeman, in an excellent article, wrote the following:

> "Herein is the crux of the problem. The seeds of gender-identity confusion are often sown, grown, and come to fruition at a time when young people don't talk about anything in their lives, much less how they see themselves as boys or girls. Then we have to deal with the fact that our natural sense and perceptions (biblically speaking) are already warped and distorted due to 'the fall' and our ensuing, yet unredeemed, sinful nature. Satan is the deceiver and is thoroughly invested in keeping us confused and deluded.
>
> "Our culture also promotes a distorted and confused sexual/gender identity. In other words, the world, the flesh, and the devil are our worst enemies, each involved in keeping us in the state of confusion and unbelief that can eventually propel us toward bondage to sexual sin . . . and far away from God and His destiny for us."[29]

---

28 John White, *Eros Redeemed*, (InterVarsity Press, 1993), 144.
29 John Freeman, "Gender Confusion," (*Harvest News Publication*, Spring, 1985), 1-2.

Here Comes Tootsie!

The question is often raised, "What about drag queens? Are they homosexual, mixed up heterosexuals, bi-sexual, transgenders, or what?"

These men perform publicly in pseudo-women's roles. Although they imitate women, they do not necessarily want to be or to live as one. Many take female hormones to enhance their external feminine appearance. Many have breast implants. They engage in their behavior primarily to obtain men's attention, love, and sexual gratification.

They are usually men struggling with their sexual identity, not their gender identity. They are "okay" with being a man, but do not feel complete as one. Dressing as a woman is their way of attaining male attention and "love." Their compelling drives are primarily homosexually oriented. They typically feel so bad about themselves as males that it's inconceivable for them to imagine receiving a man's love unless they're acting like a woman. Many of them have told me about their intense dislike of women, because women are in direct competition with them for available men. They see themselves at a distinct advantage because they can so easily relate to men (being one) and can offer men what many consider the best of both worlds.

It has been common for such men to obtain secondary female sexual characteristics primarily through the ingestion of female hormones, but not actually going so far as to have their male genitalia removed. However, today's trend, to add to their bag of tricks, is a false vaginal opening, while leaving their male genitals completely intact. This allows them to have sexual relations with both sexes. This kind of surgical procedures is called "designer sex." We indeed owe much to the creative genius of today's medical community. Thanks a lot, folks!

These men are typically discovered in gay bars, parades, theaters, strip bars—or floating motionless, face down in a turbulent river. Listen to the story of a former drag-queen, Elliot:

"Dressing as a woman gave me the popularity and acceptance I craved. I was proud to be a female impersonator. The ability to be beautiful became all that mattered in my life. My parents divorced when I was five. My dad took my sister Valerie and me to the park, knelt down beside us and told us goodbye. It was a traumatic day I'll never forget. For the rest of my childhood, I lived with the continuous insecurity that the people I loved would always be walking out of my life.

"I felt terribly insecure and different around other boys. I just could not measure up to their expectations, and, because I wasn't good in sports and was effeminate, they called me names like 'fag, queer, and sissy'. I started drinking alcohol at fourteen years of age. From the start, my goal was to get drunk, to numb the pain inside and provide temporary escape from my feelings of self-hatred and inadequacy. Due to my poor self-image, I started working with an all-night escort service as a male prostitute. I was dropped off at hotel rooms to sell my body for eighty dollars an hour.

"Another significant event happened in my life when I saw a male friend in a gay bar, dressed like a woman. His feminine appearance looked so real, but I couldn't believe it. I was fascinated and one night he put makeup and wig on me. When I looked into the mirror, I was astonished to see a beautiful 'woman' looking back at me. That night I got high and went to the bar. My real identity was hidden. No one knew it was me under the 'mask'. That night completely changed my life. Over the next three years I threw everything into being the best woman I could. I was proud to be a drag queen and adopted the name Robin. I quickly became popular in the realm of female impersonation.

"In that world, the ability to be beautiful and look convincing as a woman was all that mattered. Others told me I was one of the best, and my reputation began spreading to the neighboring states. But, inside, I still hated myself, and one night while on the dance floor I said to God, 'I know you can help me. Someday I will come back to you.' But being an excellent female impersonator was the only pride I had. The concept of being loved for just being me was totally incomprehensible."[30]

Another former drag queen, Michael, recounts that the main reason he became a female impersonator was for the attention, affirmation, and affection he was shown at the night clubs in which he performed as Michelle Danielle. He said that in his first public stage appearance he was accepted for the first time in his lifetime. And he (understandably) loved it.

---

30 John Paulk, *Love in Action Newsletter*, "Taking off the Mask," 1993.

In *Michelle Danielle is Dead*, a book about his life, Michael remarked:

> "The drag queens are into role playing. They dress
> as women and don't want to admit they are gay.
> 'I'm really a woman trapped inside a man's body.'
> The gay scene is a means to escape from reality or
> responsibility. It is a mask to hide behind. They
> want somebody else to take care of them. They
> are afraid to relate to a woman on a man-to-man
> basis. Frustration is their middle name. The drag
> queens have a lot of fear and envy . . . eaten up
> with resentment . . . very ungrateful . . . and take
> and take and take without ever a thought of giving.
> After getting high, they want to go out and pick up
> somebody. In many cases three to four days later
> they're found tied to a bed and beaten to death. It
> happens all the time."[31]

---

31 Marie S. Rice, *Michelle Danielle is Dead*, (Jonathan Publishers, 1985), 27.

Chapter 6

What about Hermaphrodites?

Hermaphrodite is not a medical term in its origin. It's actually derived from the name of a Greek god, Hermaphroditus. This heathen conceptualization of a half-and-half deity was later used to describe infants who were born with an altered chromosomal arrangement and who possessed to some degree the sexual organs of both the male and female.

In today's culture the term "intersexed person" has replaced the term "hermaphrodite." This individual suffers from a most unfortunate genetic defect that produces secondary sexual identity characteristics that are ambiguous or incongruous to the actual genetic encoding. These conditions are manifested beneath the heading of hermaphroditism, such as Turner's Syndrome (XO), Klinefelter Syndrome (XXY); and ambiguous genitalia developmental conditions such as, Adrenogenital syndrome, Androgen Insensitivity Syndrome and Reductase Deficiency Syndrome, to name a few.

It's often very apparent what the person's dominant sexual identity was designed by determining the structure of the chromosomes.

> "Analyzing a blood sample is a possible aid to specifying the true sex of such individuals as it may identify their chromosomes. Males have the sex chromosome XY; females XX."[32]

However, in some few cases, it's a tough call by physicians to determine which direction to take. The predominant sexual identity is

---

32 S. Marc Breed Love, "Sex on the Brain," (*Science Today Journal,* July 1198), 14.

generally determined by blood studies on chromosomal and endocrine levels. But in the context of this book, these individuals do not factor into our discussion. That is another subject in itself, and one I'm not going to address here. Transgenders *do not* fit within this classification, for they are typically not born with ambiguous genitalia. The confusion in the heart of the transgender is not biologically or medically induced; it is of psychological and spiritual origin. It's sufficient to say that in hermaphrodites, medical and surgical corrections can more closely bring the external genitalia into proper alignment with the God-given genetic encoding.

God's Call

I contend that our gender is assigned by our Creator at conception, male or female. Human anatomical construction is intended to fully comply with the architectural blueprint; but due to the present state of a world in chaos, we, unfortunately, do witness aberrant anatomical malformations of many kinds. It's important to remember these maladies are a result of the departure from the created order of the things way back in some remote garden. They're not the result of God's mistaken design or of indifference. It's amazing that more do not occur, with all that is at risk in the womb. Nevertheless, hormonal and chromosome mix-ups can usually be rectified through properly applied medical/surgical intervention.

The following is a personal letter from one sister to another that helps clarify what is otherwise a very complicated issue for the uninformed (used with permission). Remember that the term hermaphrodite refers to someone who is born with either both sets of genitalia, or has ambiguous genitals, making it difficult to ascertain the correct birth sex. *Intersex* is the twenty-first century term meaning the same thing.

Dear Judy,

I am sorry it has taken me so long to write back to you. I did not feel I should write back without some knowledge on the subject of transgender/intersex people. I did not want to rely only on what you told me . . . and I did not want to rely only on what I felt, so I went out on an educational tour, you might say. I wanted to be objective (if possible) but realistic at the same time. I have been in touch with organizations whose main focus is homosexuality/transgender issues. These organizations can all be found on the Internet and have vast amounts of information and people to speak with. I also spoke with my minister about Bible verses you chose to use because you know we sometimes take meaning of the Bible so literally when in fact is means something else.

I have done a lot of work here. I have spoken to numerous people, written a few letters and researched as best I could. I did this because you are my sister. I love you and I want to understand best I can, and I want to help you. You and I have always been close, and even when we were at odds, we were still more aware of each other than we were any of the other seven siblings. Why now would I say anything to make you unhappy? Why would I say anything to split us apart? You said it was fear that motivated my reactions to your condition; you should know me better than that. You also said that I don't know God or at least not like you do.

Well, my prayer is that God will let you see the truth and, although He always gives the freedom to choose, I pray He does not give you over to your choice just yet. Before I comment on each part of your letter, I want you know there is a test you can take. It is called a chromosome study.

This test will leave no doubt as to whether you are male, female, or hermaphrodite. If you really want to know the truth you will have this test done. With so much at stake, this is important. Also, your claim that an elevated testosterone level indicates that you are really a male has no validity.

A hormone test does not mean anything. It simply gives your hormone levels; a man can have low testosterone levels and a female can have high testosterone levels, but this doesn't mean anything. I'm told by multiple sources that hormone levels are not an indicator, nor can they serve as proof for a basis of considering one's gender. However, there is a lot of money at stake here and if the chromosome study was used, there would no way any doctor could prove a male was a female or a female was male.

It would be irrefutable, and the one seeking reassignment would first have to face the fact that he was indeed male or she was in fact female. You opened your letter about transgender /intersex people and then started talking about eunuchs, describing yourself as one. Regardless what that old medical textbook says, they are not one and the same. Three doctors I have consulted would agree to this and their definitions are clearly the same: "Being a eunuch does not inherently make a man into a woman. It only means that he no longer has a sex-drive and the ability to gain an erection or impregnate a woman." So, how is it that you can refer yourself as a eunuch? Maybe because you had a hysterectomy you're saying you're now a eunuch. I don't know. In either case let's go over the biblical reference you made to the same. You said that you believe God created transgender or intersex people or eunuchs. Yes, in some cases babies are born with ambiguous genitalia, (intersex), while some are born without testes, which makes them eunuchs. But to attribute these biological and genetic flaws to the creative handiwork of God is in itself a huge error (Mathew 19:12 (paraphrase).

1. **"There are eunuchs who are born that way from their mothers' wombs…"**

True: This would refer to babies born without testicles or ovaries (for female). Now you said during one of our conversations that you may have had testicles at birth. If that is the case, you would not be eunuch, but you would be a hermaphrodite. The expert I spoke with assures me that Mom would clearly have known and it would be unmistakable to you, even now. But in the cases where Hermaphrodism is suspected, a simple chromosome study could prove it.

2. *"Eunuchs who were made eunuchs by men..."*

True: Of course! We know of kings who used eunuchs to watch over their queen and their concubines. Anyway, these eunuchs had no sexual drive and thereby the king had no worries concerning relations between the eunuchs and the women. But this did not make them women. They were men who were responsible to guard over the king's prized possessions.

3. *"Eunuchs who made themselves eunuchs for the sake of the kingdom of heaven."*

True: This was about men who swore themselves to celibacy for the sake of the kingdom of God. They had one less thing to worry about. But his does not have anything to do with you either.

4. *"He who is able to accept this, let him accept it."*

I can accept this Judy. Can you accept this as well? You are not a eunuch. Transgender /intersex… Yes! Probably. We will get to that later. Regardless of what that old medical book said (and how old was it?). It was incorrect. Find a medical book, look up that page and compare it with what Christian and non-Christian doctors alike are saying about transgenderism.

Then you mentioned Acts 8:26:39. I think you have missed the point here. The Ethiopian eunuch story was about a person who happened to be a eunuch, yes, but it was not about his being a eunuch. It was about him learning of the good news that Jesus Christ, the Messiah, had come. He did not understand what he was reading and along comes Phillip out of nowhere and explains this wonderful thing—plus Phillip baptized him. The Ethiopian had much to rejoice about and he did rejoice. Who cares that he's a eunuch? It matters not. The verse you made up, "So go and be a eunuch no more," really has no bearing on the story. However there is a verse where Jesus says, "Now, go and sin no more." Now that is a verse that has meaning for all of us.

Enough about Eunuchs. Let's go on to transgenderism.

You have a choice. You may not think you do because of the depth of the situation, but you do. I know it would not be easy to make the choices against yourself and our self-declared condition, but life does not seem to offer many painless paths for any of us anyway.

5. "*To disagree to conform between a biological and the self-declared…*"

To disagree is an opinion, a thought, and finally a decision. To conform is something much bigger. This means to yield, to agree, to submit, or to obey. So we should say (and those study results say) transgender/

intersex people refuse to (or don't want to) agree with or submit to their actual biological being because they have declared themselves to be the opposite.

I remember you saying that you prayed every night that God would make you a boy. You prayed and prayed. I cannot image how let down you must have felt when it seemed that God did not listen. Well, as you know, God listens to all our prayers. Has it yet dawned on you that God, like our parents have often done, is saying, 'No!" Is it possible that God made you a girl and wanted you to be female for His plan? Of course you won't know what that plan is because you refuse to accept what God wants and are truly accepting of only that which you want. You cannot see life any other way. You cannot listen to anyone if they are telling you anything contrary to what you want to hear. Especially since becoming that boy (now a man) is within your grasp. Well, I want to tell you a couple things, and I hope you're listening:

1. You can opt for gender-reassignment if you want. No matter what changes are made on the outside, you will still be and have the genetic makeup of a female.

2. God has given us free will. We're free to choose our own beliefs, free to make our own decisions. If we're on the wrong path, He tries to teach us and reach us through all types of means. Eventually, we will do exactly what we want to do, as will you in this case. I'm not talking about sin and everyday life. Sure, we all sin, and hopefully we repent and are truly sorry. What I'm saying is that when we refuse to listen to God, refuse to honor Him for who He is, and His order for our lives, we then face serious consequences. You said I should go about fellowship with God. Well, we can (like you said) talk to Him and pray to Him, yes! But when we do, our knees should be bent and our head bowed and our heart ready to listen and obey. He is not on our level, Judy. You can tell Him our heart, but you cannot tell Him what you will do and won't do. He's very specific, and the Bible says He shows no favoritism. When God makes Himself plain to people—when they don't listen and instead do what they want (freedom of choice)—He give them over them over to their desires.

Romans 1:18-25 speaks of people who know God and yet refuse to acknowledge Him, refuse to bow before Him. People know Him yet allow themselves to be led astray. It speaks of those who suppress the truth (this sounds to me like "refusing to conform"). He also says very directly that, "The truth is known to them because He (God) Himself has made it plain to them." In this there is no misunderstanding. He is speaking of people who know His invisible qualities, eternal power, and divine nature. But later it says, "They exchanged the truth of God for a lie." This is very important: It says, "You, therefore, have no excuse" (Romans 1:2).

Do you know why they are without excuse? It's because they knew what they were doing was wrong and with their own free choice they nevertheless blatantly chose against God's will. So God gave them over to their own desires. That sounds mighty scary to me. It sounds very final.

Back to your letter: What does repentance mean? The act of turning away from sin and changing one's previous orientation form rebellion against God . . . to an acceptance of His will. You cannot sin on purpose, secretly holding the thought, "I'll sin now (thinking all sin is forgiven anyway), and then repent later". It doesn't work that say. That's kind of like spitting in God's eye.

You said you believe you were altered at birth. Well, I'm told that the chromosome study will tell you once and for all if that's true. Plus, I cannot imagine why you would not want to speak with more people about this. You said that I base my decisions on fear. This is one of the few things you said that made me very angry, because you know that is not true form the way I have lived my life with you. I was afraid to write you the first letter. But I wrote it anyway. And regardless of the path you take, I will always be your sister, your friend, and your listener (if you're still listening to me). I am not going anywhere. When you initially called to tell me about all of this stuff, I didn't have any answers. After much prayer and lots of secular and Christian input, it seems as though all of the answers have snapped together like pieces to a puzzle. But now that I've learned things that are contrary to what you've expressed or what you might think, you want to be angry and quickly disregard what I've discovered, saying my motives for doing so are all based on fear. You've been snide, sarcastic, and nasty to me. To those things, I have no comment. I want to help you. You can be helped, if you want to be. But you've aligned yourself with a network of people who are supportive and who stand by you, and that's gotta feel good. But in the long run, it's going to be bad. How many of them will base their opinions on God's blueprint, God's plans? That's very important! I'm going to close now because I only wanted to give you the facts as they referred to the letter you wrote me. If you can refute what I've written, please do so. The first thing I want refuted is that you are female, because we know that there is a conclusive test to prove if you are a female, male, or hermaphrodite. If I were you, I would want to be sure. I'm only looking out for your best interest, and I hope you would do the same for me. You're my sister. I love you (miss you, too). No one can convict me for not caring; that's for sure.

—Your sister

It's important to understand that one of the main arguments today from the individual struggling with conflicting sexual and gender-identity issues is caused from their self-view. They offer their self-diagnosed condition, stating that they are a product of a freak accident of nature, which is best corrected through surgical intervention.

Stephan protests:

> "I'm either a hermaphrodite or at the least a
> pseudo-hermaphrodite, because I feel like a
> woman trapped in a male body."

One male-to-female transgender confessed:

> "I presented myself to the doctor as a hermaph-
> rodite, showing him a large and imposing scar
> on my scrotum, telling him that it was where
> the vaginal opening was located at the time
> of birth. It was actually a botched-up surgical
> procedure on my undescended testicles."

This line of reasoning sounds convincing to the unknowledgeable bystander, sometimes even to the physicians. This, of course, is the objective. Confusion begets confusion.

Brainwashed

The transgender community has cleverly promoted the theory that the brain of the male fetus, which normally undergoes a brain-washing of testosterone during the first months of formation, has somehow been insufficiently bathed. They conclude that when the brain does not experience this washing, the boy will then have a dominant female brain structure, which explains his conflicting desires to fulfill the feminine role.

Of course, any medical/geneticist specialist who does not have a self-serving socio/political bias will admit that such theories are exactly that—theories! No conclusive studies have been done or replicated to support beliefs that transgenderism or homosexuality are genetically or chemically caused.

Updated reports conducted by Dr. S. Marc Breedlove of the University of California recently discovered the morphological differences between the brains of humans with different sexual orientation/gender identity indicate that the casual chain as well as actual brain structures are dramatically changed or altered by sexual behavior alone.

My conclusion is that recently concocted, scientifically manufactured theories are simply another attempt to place the blame for one's choices upon the "fickle finger of fate," as opposed to simply being honest. But we've seen the evidence that "If you tell a lie often enough, it will eventually be believed." All such theories have one goal: to rationalize or explain abnormal (rebellious) behavior. After all, none of us wants to feel different. How does a guy explain his secret desire to wear women's clothes, or the sense that there is a female presence trapped inside his body? It's consoling to do some kind of scientific study (manipulated as it may be), to help alleviate the necessity to take personal responsibility for our sinful actions.

Oswald Chambers wrote,

> "The old Puritan idea that the devil tempts men
> has this remarkable effect; it produced the man
> of iron who fought. The modern idea of blaming
> his heredity or his circumstance produces the man
> who succumbs at once."[33]

---

33 Oswald Chambers, *My Utmost for His Highest*, (Dodd & Mead, 1935), 127.

In our refusal to take personal responsibility, we protest. Let's place all of this on God's doorstep! He's to blame because He took a break at the crucial moment when my brain was to have been "bathed" with testosterone (the stuff that would have given me a man's brain). Instead, I'm now stuck with a woman's brain inside my cranium. It was God's failure. "Thanks a lot, God!" Such reasoning was a part of Adam's initial rebellion. It's pretty lame-brained thinking, isn't it? We're accustomed to bending our knees to the gods of science, believing that if a "scientific inquiry" turns up some kind of theoretical proposition, then it must be so. Add to that the further propagation of lies by the press and we have a sure recipe for echoing misinformed conclusions.

Even if one day, legitimate scientific inquiry were to prove that genetically imposed conditions make one predisposed to sexual/gender identity confusion, I would not be disheartened.

A discovery of the cause of this disorder does not validate one's acceptance of it. Billions of dollars are currently being spent in the field of genetic engineering. Researchers are taking diseased genes and subjecting them to vast assortments of procedures in the attempt to see which one destroys the malfunctioning gene.

We go to great measures to explore possibilities of preventing malformations, believing that genetic predispositions to cancer, Alzheimer's, or any other disease should be altered, if possible. A treatment should be sought.

Why is it that when it comes to gender-identity issues that science seems willing to hopelessly acquiesce rather than find a cure? We cannot bypass the obvious if we're truly trying to find answers to the difficulties surrounding transgender desires. There still exists overwhelming evidence that one's natural social environs plays a critical role in the final outcome. Sound too Freudian for you? Sorry. The facts constantly point to the family and social surroundings as the key elements in the formation of these neuroses or psychoses. There are millions of choices, but one thing is sure: There is ultimately only one person responsible for who I've become: ME!

Truths and Choices

- We didn't know the addictive effect when masturbating with mom's panties.

- It's true that we never invited that unwanted molestation.

- We didn't choose the family we had to live with . . . or without.

- We didn't choose our physical stature or our basic personality traits.

- We didn't choose to be called a "sissy" because we liked to play with dolls.

But this does not exempt us from being responsible for who we've become today. The final determining factor does not rest on what happened to us, but on how we responded to those events. What choices have we made as a result? Have we tenaciously held on to bitter judgments against those who inured us, or have we come to a place of forgiveness? Have we nurtured the lies about our person-hood, or have we replaced them with the truth about us that Jesus Christ imparts by direct revelation through His Word and His holy presence? The mistake so often made is administering a self-made anesthetic agent (the coping mechanisms of cross dressing), in order to feel good again. Willingly participating in the forbidden eventually leads to constant obsessions, eventual overdoes, and perhaps death.

Developing the False Feminine Identity: A Process

One of my defining choices was made at the ripe old age of three-and-a-half. I'd already acquired a taste for feeling the false feminine. My palate was tantalized with the sweetness of those experiences in which Mother playfully dressed me in girl's things. However, thirteen years later she didn't find it so amusing.

Upon discovering me at the age of sixteen, fully dressed in her things, she asked, "Are you obsessed with this because I used to dress you up like the girl I wanted to have?" Not until that moment did she possibly come to understand the seriousness of the seemingly innocent play of years past. She never realized she was affirming the false feminine in me. If she had, she wouldn't have done it.

How could she have known that her innocent fantasies were becoming my own? My hard drive joyfully installed the text, "When doing this, I feel cute, loveable, and close to Mommy."

By the age of three-and-a-half, I was convinced that it was the best way to get her attention, and I loved that special feeling of being uniquely linked to her and her comfortable world. Like many other children at that age, not yet able to discern which sex we really are, I desired most to be like her. I wanted to be (a distinct choice) her little girl. I wanted to be like the girls in the neighborhood, especially my next-door neighbor Susie. Susie and I spent lots of time together playing with our dollies and having all kinds of fun. My mother, of course, naively validated that. So did my father.

I remember sitting on the front porch of my home at the age of three, playing dolls with Susie. We were having the best time. She was extending to me her doll, and with that exchange, I took more than the doll. I sealed inside my little heart an alter identity by my earnest vow that I was going to be like Susie. I was going to be like her mother, and I was going be like my mommy. I was going to be a part of that soft, enticing, feminine world. I'd already figured out that I didn't want to be a part of my dad's world. I didn't even like him; he was unknowable intrusion in my life. It wasn't that Dad was a bad person. He just wasn't appealing to me. Some of the other men in my life were equally distasteful. They were rough handling, gruff talking, and bad smelling, and they did things I disliked.

Separation Anxiety

But Mommy? Well, that is clearly another story. I really liked to be around her when she was home. I know that I suffered from separation anxiety by the very nature of the fact she would leave for work early in the morning, and I would not see her until just before bedtime. I was stuck with Grandma all day long.

The term *separation anxiety* is clearly spelled out in *Boundaries* by Cloud and Townsend:

> "Bonding takes place when the mother responds
> to the needs of the child, the needs for closeness,
> for being held, for food, and for changing. As
> baby experiences needs and the mother's positive
> response to those needs, he or she begins to inter-

nalize, or take in, an emotional picture of a loving and constant mother. Babies, at this stage, have no sense of self apart from mother. They think, 'Mommy and me are the same.' It's sometimes called symbiosis, a sort of 'swimming in closeness' with Mother. This symbiotic union is the reason babies panic when Mother is not around. No one can comfort them but their mother."[34]

So, before the age of four I had already determined I was going to be like Mommy. It was not just a matter of play. I had made a life decision. Susie and I went all the way through elementary and high school together. She as my closet friend, and I always felt good in her presence. We had good times as "girls."

Then the bombshell dropped! Dressing in Mommy's things was commonplace before I started kindergarten. But on the morning of my first day of school, I distinctly remember my mother sitting on the edge of my bed. The features of her face are blurred, sort of like those on television coverage of police arrest when criminal's facial features are totally distorted to protect their anonymity. That's how I visualize Mom's face that dreadful day. Her voice is garbled but the message is loud and clear. She's informing me that I will no longer be able to wear girls' dresses since I am going to school. She's holding up a pair of boys' slacks, showing them to me, telling me that this is the kind of clothing that I'm going to have to wear all the time.

Shame slapped me in the face full force! This is the first time I was told it was wrong for me to wear dresses. At that point I'm ashamed

---

34 Henry Cloud and John Townsend, *Boundaries*, (Zondervan, 1996), p. 67.

for wanting to dress like Susie, or for identifying with Mother by dressing like her. It was very confusing, to say the least.

Oh how I hated my first day of school. Separation from Mommy would have been enough, but to compound that devastation, I went off to school beneath the unbearable weight and confusion of shame. There simply are no words to describe that kind of internal anguish. My soul felt like someone had lifted the hatch and lobbed in a grenade, leaving me totally fragmented. I'd been all ready to go to kindergarten and have fun with the girls, as I was accustomed to doing, dressing and playing like them, emulating our mommies, and our favorite people. My world was never the same.

The Accusation: Worthless

One of our most debilitating enemies is shame. Scribed upon the side of the deadly projectile are these words: "You are so despicable, so unwanted, so unlovable, and so twisted that you might as well kill yourself. The world would be far better off without the likes of you! You are at the core of your miserable being a worthless person. There is no remedy for you."

Once delivered, received, and believed, its deadly effects are guaranteed—unless countermeasures are employed. In order to survive, you must devise another plan. The countermeasure commonly used is the cover up. Feeling very much like an espionage agent, you begin deceiving through unending lies, always fearful of being discovered, constantly looking over your shoulder, wondering if anyone detects what's going on inside your heart.

Then something begins to happen that makes the cover up even more difficult. Others your age begin segregating; dividing off from those they once enjoyed spending time with. Girls stick up their noses and boys hold theirs. I greeted this stage of my boyhood with protest: "Wait a minute, I like being with my girlfriends." That's when Bobby called me "sissy." I wanted to be like the guys, but did it mean that I could not be like my very best friends anymore?

"Individuation"

My family doctor would have referred to this period of childhood development as "individuation." At this stage of development we are merely trying to grow into our own individual identity apart from our parents. By the time we're catching the school bus for the first grade, the process of individuation has begun.

There's nothing wrong with a little guy playing with girls' things. He's not able to make clear-cut distinctions as to what or who he is until much later, unless he's feeling so bad about himself, or the male role models around him, that he begins to regularly dissociate himself from them and their world. Playing with dolls or Mommy's lipsticks at the age of two or three is normal childhood play. But if he's doing it when he's in the second grade, there is strong indication of an enemy in the camp!

When the kindergarten boy is in the process of individuating, he's trying to accomplish this God-given task of exploring and learning to function in his daddy's world. What happens when he attempts to scale the wall into Daddy's world only to be repelled by criticism, rejection, and hurtful comments? What if he finds Daddy unappealing, too threatening, un-affirming, and unloving? Chances are he'll make a steady retreat into the soft, safe, and nurturing arms of Mommy. Who can blame the little guy for that?

All kinds of war stories exist when investigating the little boy's reactions to his dad's world. One of the most common is the defensive position. The boy's siblings and mother have spent lots of time huddling together in their bunker, shielding themselves from yet another assault of their common enemy. "Oh, great, Dad's in another bad mood. He's taking it all out on us. Worst of all, he left bruises on Mommy's cheek. I hate him! Another story that is all too prevalent is that of the father who was demonstrative in his love for his wife and daughters, but paid little attention to his son. Dad's emotional detachment comes across to the son as harsh, demeaning, or critical—and sometimes it is.

Listen to Jim's comments:

> "Dad always called me names, saying that I was stupid or unable to do what real men could do. He could not see the value in my mom's insistence that I take piano lessons when it was so important to him that I play in a baseball league. Mom knew that I was musically talented, but all Dad could see was that I was letting him down, at least that is how I think he felt."

Dangerous Affirmation

Many men I know have also related how their father strongly affirmed them when they were dressed in girls' clothing. An all-too-common scenario is this: Here you have a small tyke carrying the heavy load of shame and masculine inadequacy around his neck, and he's given the opportunity to dress like a girl for a Halloween party. His mom and older sister meticulously help him primp for the night out. He stumbles on the stilts (called high heels) as he makes his way through the living room, where his Dad is numbed out in front of his television. Normally his presence would go undetected since he and his Dad don't have a lot in common. He's normally referred to as "Mommy's boy." But what is about to happen is like stepping on a land mine. Dad's TV stupor is interrupted by his son's intrusion. Mindlessly, he exclaims, "Wow, you sure make a pretty girl! We always wished you were one!" He then turns back to the cowboy movie he's seen a hundred times, as though there is nothing better to do.

His explosive comment blasts the confused kid's heart to sheds; he's left reeling, but not from his balancing act on top of the heels. A trail of emotional blood follows him out the door. "For once," he mutters to himself, "Dad paid attention to me, even complimented me, I liked that feeling. I bet that is how my sister feels all the time. Lucky her!" He then fantasizes more and eventually embraces what is called a "false feminine" identity, carefully guarded in a lockbox, labeled "top secret." Though it emerges more and more regularly, his trips into mom's closet normally remain well concealed, especially from dad. If detected, the results would most likely be too devastating to deal with, so the child learns well how to move in shame-filled darkness, performing his secret missions under the cover of the night. Although his deepest, unfulfilled longing is to have his father's love, affirmation, and undivided attention, he finally aborts the mission. The impenetrable wall around dad defies any of his tactical maneuvers. He returns, or remains in his mothers' protective embrace, by wrapping himself in that which represents her: her clothing.

Although the boy idolizes his mother, he continues to suffer from his unwanted separation from her. Yes, he has found himself drawn to wear that which represents her. He dresses like her and desperately tries to emulate her. He may even takes measures to assure a permanent likeness to her through surgical (cosmetic) alteration of bodily tissue, but a paradox remains forcefully intact.

The Mother They Never Really Knew

The paradox is this: I have discovered a common story after hundreds of hours counseling men who really believed they and their mothers were close. I personally relate to the truth of it: The son doesn't really know his mother. He is bonded to her only through her clothing, or that which reminds him of her. I was shocked with the eventual revelation of how little I genuinely knew my mom.

An individual recently shared that he now realizes that he was trying to "remain bonded with his 'mother' through the privacy of her closet." The imagined close relationship with Mother is usually not as solid as one would expect.

The personal experience of Ricky is additional proof of this:

> "I did not know her. I thought I did. Everyone
> else thought I did. We did lots of things together.
> We even bore close physical resemblance.
> I thought like her, even reflected her manner-
> isms, but I didn't really know who my mom was.
> I just believed I did because I was so in love with
> the idea of being like her. Most painful has been
> the discovery that I harbored secret resentment
> in my heart toward her for having left me. I feel
> so tricked and confused by it all."

Most mothers have an innate, attractive pull of affirmation, of being protective, and of feminine nurturing. But staying in such an environment, not venturing away from that haven into the adventurous, risky, often threatening world of the father, leaves the boy inwardly knowing he has lacked something crucial in his development. His defensive detachment from father and periodic visits to mother's things further locks him in the closet of deepening shame and loss. The boy is sure of his intense love for mom. But what he has really come to know and love is his imagined connection with her. His emotional umbilical cord is not yet severed. Being with her through wearing her things seems to be enough. It isn't.

A remarkably high percentage of men involved in transgender behavior will, in the climactic moment of their cross-dressing escapade, ejaculate directly into the article of women's clothes they've worn. It is a habitual ritual for many, especially when in the early stages of puberty and adolescence. The men have little, if any, understanding of why they do that. I've discovered that it's a subconscious way of preventing the "false feminine" from totally conquering their entire personality. There's enough residual masculine spunk left in them to resist total occupation. By masturbating into women's clothing, they are able to prove their innate manhood, even though their outward appearance is feminine. It is a form of masculine protest. The brainwashing happens all right, but the kind that produces transgender desires is of another cause than the womb experience: The child's perceptions and self-view are foundationally erected by parents, family, friends, teacher, peers, and world opinion. It's all about how one thinks about himself that makes the difference, which is the direct result of how he has viewed himself through the lenses of significant others.

Chapter 7

He Understands

Our sense of being, as mentioned earlier, is vulnerable to attack in this foreign environment called Earth. From the very beginning of His earthly trek, Jesus Himself suffered in the same ways we do (see Philippians 2:5-8; Hebrews 2:14-18). He came not only to redeem our lives, but to teach us how to live. He was tempted in every way that we are, yet did not enter into doing sinful things (see Hebrews 4:15). Jesus' entire life was a series of put downs, rejections, and criticisms, even from His immediate family. Yet He chose not to retaliate or let those things deter Him from deeply and truly loving those who had so severely mistreated Him. Forgiveness and love propelled His course. He did not permit the devil or any other person to prevent Him from being a magnificent role model for us. He really does understand our pain. He has eternal wounds to prove it.

Jesus' sense of well-being was nourished by being close to His earthly father and His Heavenly Father. Ideally, we should find our well-being in the same way; it should be profoundly influenced first by our earthy father's involvement in our life, and then eventually released into the care of our intimate Heavenly Father. Too often that is not the case.

For me, connecting with my dad was aborted by puberty. He did not understand me, and I did not want to know him. Mom was my heroine (remember, my story represents hundreds). As I became profoundly aware of the chasm developing between Dad and me—and even with Mom (because of her beauty shop)—I found myself daily and compulsively drawn to Mom's wardrobe, to things that represented her to me. I would hide my mothers' things in my room, not giving a thought to the possibility that she would miss her slip the next day. As a kid, I was unable to see things from her perspective. What pain she must have suffered when she realized that her clothes were disappearing.

One day, when I was in puberty, I came home to discover Mom and my brother busily cleaning out my closet. Mom had found my private stash of her missing things in a corner of the closet. Many of the items were soiled and dirty, smeared with lipstick and other obvious indicators of a major problem in her eldest son's life. She held up one of her under slips, remarking, "Well, I wondered where my things had gone!" The cat was out of the bag! I immediately high-tailed it out of the house in total embarrassment and shame, licking my wounds for quite some time before returning home. I did not know what fate awaited me. Nothing came of it.

I remember secretly wishing that Mom and Dad would intervene and help me, even though that prospect scared me. But family secrets don't usually find the light of the day. They stayed just that— secrets! Mom never talked to me about it. It was as though it never happened, which was our typical family response. Our family motto was, "If you don't talk about it, then it will eventually take care of itself." From then on, I became far more careful about handling mom's things, learning to return every item just as I'd found it.

Brief Review

First: By the age of three-and-a-half, I'd already decided that I was going to be like my mom and other girls. I'd adopted the feminine name other girls had given me, identifying myself as Carol Ann, rather than by my birth name.

Second: I began to *defensively-detach* myself from all the men around me, even from those who hadn't hurt me. I did not like, trust, or want to be around men. I was not very interested in anything they did. I was not at all interested in sports, fishing, hunting, or any number of things that were drawing cards for normal boys.

Third: There was a *separation between mother and me,* which resulted in untold anxiety. Most would automatically assume that transgender desires are chiefly the result of the boy's over bonding with his mother. That would seem to make sense, and is often the case. If the little fellow is obsessively dressing in mother's things, he obviously is overly bonded with her, right? Yes and No. It also attests to the boy's lack of bonding, or his refusal to disconnect with Mom, playing itself out in his attempts to *bond instead with his idea of mother,* typified by her clothing.

Forth: Mom's world is *preferred,* and womanhood becomes an idolatrous form of worship.

Fifth: *Further bonds develop with that which represent mother*—her clothing. Just being dressed like her is like taking a slice of homemade bread, fresh out of the oven. I enjoyed her company, mainly because she was interested in my day, asked questions, and rubbed my neck while I shared with her some of the things that happened at school. We were connected in that way. I was not bonded with her, but bonded with that which represented her—in her absence. I regularly cried as I dressed in Mom's things, wishing and even praying that someday I could be just like her. "Somehow there must be a way."

Restoring the Soul

In order to be restored and disentangled from the disabling conditions of homosexuality or transgender confusion, we have to allow the Great Physician to do His work. He will enter with us into those troublesome memories, divide truth from error, and do what only He can do—joyfully affirm our gender-identity.

Many of us can easily relate to the following all-too-common childhood reflection offered up in one of Leanne Payne's resources:

> " . . . his feelings of being 'castrated, emasculated, weak, queer, twisted' were continually strengthened by the father who remained distant and by the mother who, when functioning at all, pampered him in the extreme. To her, he was a helpless, hurting appendage of herself, a self that was narcissistic, depressed, and utterly passive."[35]

Our identity became so tied to Mother that we find it nearly impossible to separate ourselves from the emotional umbilicus. We are suspended by this tether throughout our life, with the unfortunate climatic end of being suffocated by it. The pain involved in the inner awareness that your sexual identity is not satisfactory is more than a child can successfully handle.

---

35 Payne, Leanne. *Crisis in Masculinity* (p. 24). Baker Publishing Group. Kindle Edition.

> "Before we are six, the ability later to enjoy our sex
> cannot enter into the fullness of what ought to be.
> Aberrational forms subsequently await us like reefs
> under the shallow waters of our living."[36]

Don't be afraid, for Christ is there to take you firmly through to a safe landing place. He will often give you the opportunity to enter into healing prayer with a trusted friend or counselor who can be "Jesus with skin on" to you. Many times it is too frightening to face the nightmarish memories alone.

Those who choose to remain in the familiar confines of the status quo of their arrested emotional development and resultant sin are only going to find solace in parroting irresponsible propaganda such as, "It's not my fault because it's genetically predisposed, a God-given condition." Or "I am what I am today because of my dad's wrongs!" These explanations are nothing more than ignoring the painful memories of our yesterdays. We are too afraid of facing the past and having to thread our way through the unknown to the other side, even though personal wholeness and restoration awaits. Many of the most traumatic or significant childhood memories evade our conscious recall. The reason:

> "No one completely understands the mental, emo-
> tional and neurological process. But we do know
> that it requires a great deal of continuous emo-
> tional and spiritual energy to keep the memory in
> its hidden place. It could be compared to a person
> trying to hold a bunch of balloons under water.

---

36 John & Paula Sanford, *The Transformation of the Inner Man*, (Victory House, 1982), 271

> "He succeeds for a while but finally runs out of
> energy; they pop up here and there in spite of his
> desperate efforts. Such repressed and fixated mem-
> ories can never really be forgotten. Nor can they
> simply be filed away in the same way our minds
> store pleasant memories with the accompanying
> good feelings. For the harder we try to keep bad
> memories out of conscious recall, the more pow-
> erful they become. Since we dare not allow them
> to enter through the door of our minds directly,
> they come into our personalities, bodies, minds
> and spirits in disguised and destructive ways. There,
> denied problems go underwater and later reappear
> as certain kinds of recurring cycles of spiritual
> defeat."[37]

I had given up ever trying to please Dad as a male, which led to a pervading sense of hopeless despair. I had an "all is lost" attitude that grew out of past hurts inflicted by careless, sometimes mean-spirited comments that proved to be too toxic to handle as an impressionable child.

It was not until I began the lengthy process of spiritual and emotional restoration that I discovered (much to my dismay) that I was keeping the pain of my yesterday's alive through cross dressing. Crossing the gender lines was not bringing the much-desired resolution to my past hurts, disappointments, and relational failures, or my consuming sense of personal insecurity and inadequacy. I was

---

37 David A. Seamands, *Healing Your Heart of Painful Emotions*, (Inspirational Press, 1993), 270

subservient to lust and unsuccessfully tending to the many festering wounds of skirmishes fought in other battles of years past.

As one wise counselor advised:

> "Though you are the product of all your yesterdays,
> if you allow God to heal you, He can change things
> so that your yesterdays no longer control your
> todays. And God will be the blessed controller of
> all of your days."[38]

To achieve personal restoration, you must accept into the mix the disruptive and pervasive healing work of God's Spirit. He knows exactly where you were hurt and how to strategize a remedy. Often He will re-live childhood memories with you, so that you bring finality to the unsettled confusion, lies, and hurtful events of the past, walking alongside of you as you work toward your emotional maturity.

Excellent resources are available for you to study in preparation for this kind of restoration. Some of the most helpful books are written by Leanne Payne, John and Paula Sanford, Gordon Dalby, Rita Bennett, Dr. Ed Smith, David Seamands, Joe Dallas, Jeffrey Satinover, and David Kyle Foster.

You will be amazed at the remarkable things Jesus does to bring healing to your damaged emotions. The Holy Spirit activates our memory bank in order to access the origin of emotional disruption for the purpose of entering into that memory—bringing His healing presence. Within a short time (in the subconscious memory) an

---

38 Rita Bennett, *Emotionally Free*, (Fleming H. Revell, 1982), 106

emotional transformation can come when the pain of the past is released to the Lord.

As one person described:

> "Memory by memory, the Lord applied His touch
> until the emotional pain was healed."[39]

That kind of work is not a one-shot deal, but an ongoing ministry in which we allow the transforming grace of our Lord to change us from the inside out.

One psychologist explains it in these words:

> "Our long-term memory is like a library. The main problem is not one of storage, but of retrieval. In early life, children code their memories in pictures, since they are creative and also don't have a developed verbal capacity. But we adults code our memories verbally, and can't remember some early events because we don't have the right card catalogue, or the picture of the early event, so it can be retrieved and relieved in Him.[40]

Let me share one such occasion when I was alone with God in prayer, trying to unravel the meaning of some troubling imagery that had been projected upon my mind during the day. I wrote this in my journal:

---

39 Fred Littauer, *The Promise of Restorations*, (Here's Life Publications, 1990), 76.
40 Rita Bennett, *Emotionally Free*, (Fleming H. Revell, 1982), 106

"All I could see were still portraits of myself, as though I was frozen in time. An assortment of these snapshot memories were reviewed that night as I slept. In a vivid dream I was walking down a busy highway dressed in a long, flowing woman's nightgown. I was afraid people were seeing it, so I desperately tried to cover it with a white linen sheet that was draped loosely about me. People would give second looks and turn from me, snickering.

"In the second part of the dream I found a large hotel and knew that I had to make my way to its fifth floor. Close acquaintances filed by me in the stairway, recognizing my obvious agitation and humiliation yet unable to discern my self-destructive intentions. I was ashamed. I finally got to the fifth floor and looked down to the ground beneath, saying to myself, 'This will do!' Then I jumped. Startled, I awakened and got up from my bed and went into my study to pray. I asked the Lord to tell me what was going on. The obvious message of walking in shame and fear of being discovered was clear. I asked the Holy Spirit to reveal the deeper meanings of the pictures in my mind. I invited Jesus to be present with me in that moment. The invitation was for Jesus to enter into my childhood events in a new and living way, giving a new shape to the wars of yesterday's gone by. I wrote about what happened; immediately a hazy black-and-white picture formed somewhere in the back crevices of my mind. I was staring at my mom's nightgown that hung on a hook on the right side of her closet. The image then became three-dimensional and brilliantly colorful, no longer captured in still portraits, but instead quite animated. I was naked and had just put on the nightgown and admiring my new look and the incredible, soothing softness. While it felt good, I also felt an accompanying rush of shame, guilt, and confusion. At that moment, I turned in response to an intruder's unexpected presence.

"It was Jesus. He stopped and extended His open arms to me. I couldn't make out His facial expression; it was blurred by the light, but I could see His hair. I was ashamed to have Him see me in the nightgown, so I made a feeble attempt to get rid of the evidence by hastily removing it and throwing it on the floor of the open chest.

"Jesus then motioned for me to come closer to Him. I ran into His arms, as any five-year-old would, burying my head deep into His welcoming chest. His chest was the most masculine one I could imagine, yet it seemed to envelop me as though it were a mother's breast. At the same time, I caught two distinctly different fragrances coming from His person: His robe was saturated with a man's body odor, and His skin smelled of the sweetest perfume. I was conscious of His masculine strength as He drew me closer into His masculine/ feminine chest and body. I was enfolded by His great love. My nakedness? Totally concealed within the safe confines of His flowing robe. I felt safe, secure, and wonderfully loved. I wept uncontrollably when I heard Him comfort me with repeated affirmations: 'It's okay, Jerry, I love you and accept you as My son.' God knew that such living affirmations were essential to my survival, growth, and restoration."

It was in this event that I finally began to connect with my true masculine self and took a significant step into freedom, experiencing a release from trying to be the person I perceived others wanted me to be. I sensed that I no longer needed to perform well enough for their approval. For such deep wounds to become healed you have no other option than to intentionally develop a deepening intimacy with our Creator through the humility of absolute honesty and willingness to become as a little child crying out for all Christ offers to genuine seekers. His only need is that we open our hearts to Him. Therein lays the major hurdle for most of us: Our trust level has been ruthlessly assaulted since we were infants. Satan has worked overtime to beat us into submission and despair.

We must take the risk of placing ourselves in the vulnerable position of confessing our sins to the Lord and opening our hearts to His timely ways of healing. The main obstacle is our impatience. It's a process, not another superficial quick fix. Inner-healing prayers, honest and open confessions, ongoing accountability, deliverance through an abundance of books—all of these things and many more have resulted in one very thankful man—a war-torn veteran returned home. The skeptic may scoff, saying, "Well, it would be nice if those kinds of things would happen to me. But, since that's never taken place, it sounds to me like a terribly overworked imagination." I readily understand that kind of cynicism. All I can say is that Jesus can and does enter into what we designate as our unchangeable history. He has a way of making all things new!

I have stated many times that there is no quick fix. I would like to share with you now some key practices to help you move forward in your personal restoration.

- Regular medical or Christian psychiatric follow up as needed

- Weekly accountability support group setting

- Regular, ongoing, specialized sexual-addiction and pastoral counseling

- Daily spiritual disciplines of devotions, personal prayer, and worship

- Daily journal keeping

- Regular ongoing reading of Christ-centered recovery resources

- Quarterly exposure to a Christian spiritual/emotional healing seminar

- Regular, weekly church attendance and Bible study

- Daily, intimate, and transparent heart-to-heart communication with your spouse (if married)

- A list of names to call for prayer and support when facing temptation

- Purposeful and intentional avoidance of old haunts

- Keeping away from places and people who serves as reminders of the past

- Direct pastoral oversight by someone on your church staff

- Giving back to newcomers what you have learned (best done after completing one year's consistent attendance and participation)

These are some of the things that will bring about an inner peace in one's relations with self, others, and God. The independent, single-handed, Lone Ranger mentality should be immediately abandoned. It hasn't done a good work up to this point, has it? Do all you can to place yourself in settings and among trusted Christian people who truly understand your concerns, those who will speak truth to your heart no matter what. This should be lifetime commitment, not just until things get better with the wife or things seem calmer. There is hope for total restoration. God is the Restorer of all things!

According to Scripture, God has a good plan for your life, (not the life you have created, filled with secrets and calamity). God's plan is to give you a bright future and expectant hope (see Jeremiah 29:11). God delights in healing us. And the way He goes about it is intensely personal. There's no such thing as a one-size-fits-all method in God's transformation process. All He asks is that we submit to His will and His ways. That's an ongoing work. Overnight changes rarely occur, because God is about the task of building Christian character, something few of us have acquired from our natural upbringing and many self-serving choices.

. . . being confident of this, that he who began a good work in you will carry it on to completion until the day of Christ Jesus.

—Philippians 1:6

As Oswald Chambers wrote,

> "The old Puritan idea that the devil tempts men had this remarkable effect, it produced the man of iron who fought; the modern idea of blaming his heredity or his circumstances produces the man who succumbs at once."[41]

---

41 Oswald Chambers, *My Utmost for His Highest*, (Dodd & Mead, 1935), p. 127.